WITHDRAWN

INVESTIGATING LINGUISTIC ACCEPTABILITY

JANUA LINGUARUM

STUDIA MEMORIAE
NICOLAI VAN WIJK DEDICATA

edenda curat

C. H. VAN SCHOONEVELD

INDIANA UNIVERSITY

SERIES MINOR
NR. LIV

1966

MOUTON & CO.

LONDON · THE HAGUE · PARIS

INVESTIGATING
LINGUISTIC
ACCEPTABILITY

by

RANDOLPH QUIRK *and* JAN SVARTVIK
LONDON   GÖTEBORG

1966
MOUTON & CO.
LONDON · THE HAGUE · PARIS

Printed in the Netherlands

ACKNOWLEDGMENTS

This study reports work conducted within the Survey of English Usage and as such it is a product of collaboration between all the members of the Survey staff. To our colleagues Henry T. Carvell (on whose help with the statistical work we have heavily relied), Derek Davy, Jo Evetts, Norman Fairclough, Judith A. Godfrey, Sidney Greenbaum, and Joan Mulholland, therefore, we wish to express our special gratitude for their co-operation from the planning of the first experiment to the completion of this report. In addition, we have profited from valuable help given by others at various stages of the work: the skilled advice of John K. Hall in analysing and presenting the data; the help of Eric Quirk in checking and correcting; the specialised criticism of Peter C. Wason from a psychological point of view. In the early stages of planning the experiment, we received important help and advice from Noam Chomsky, during his visit to London in November 1964. The debt we owe to predecessors and fellow-workers in the field of linguistic acceptability is, we trust, made sufficiently plain by the references throughout, but we should like to acknowledge additional help in private communications from David G. Hays (to whom we owe Fig. 10), Paul Ziff (who made valuable comments on a preliminary version of this study), D. L. Bolinger, and Barbara M. H. Strang.

University College London   R. Q. – J. S.
September 1965

CONTENTS

1

INTRODUCTION

'Grammaticalness' involves two prime but interrelated difficulties – establishing what it is and determining native reaction in respect of it, the interrelation entering through the obvious fact that the second is dependent on the first, the linguist's categorial problem. On the first of these, one writer has summed up the position in a light-hearted but fundamentally serious comment: 'I have been unable to find any agreement among modern linguists as to what constitutes a grammatical sentence. At one extreme there are those who call every utterance a sentence, that is any string of words ever mouthed by poet or peasant. At the other extreme there are those who would declare cannibalism ungrammatical on the grounds that *man* does not belong to the class of food-nouns' (Lambek, 1961, 167). The second difficulty has been epitomised with similar epigrammatical irony: 'Psycholinguistic material is notoriously hard to manage. Naive native speakers of Standard Average European are almost extinct' (Hays, 1964, 525).

A great deal of interest has been focussed on the problem in recent years, and it is beyond question that this interest has been aroused through the startling clarity with which 'the fundamental aim' of a grammar has been formulated by generative linguists: that it should account for 'all and only the grammatical sentences of a language' (cf. Chomsky, 1957, 13, 21; Bach, 1964, 5). What is startling here is that a tacit assumption traditional in all grammar-writing has been made explicit, and consequently we are confronted with the full implications of this assumption. The most important of these for our present purpose is not that there are the entities 'fully grammatical' and 'fully ungrammatical' sentences but that there is the ability to draw a line between the two. The confrontation makes it clear that grammatical rules which have hitherto been preoccupied with preventing the kind of deviance of which native speakers are capable

(1)   *Him and her don't want no cake.*

or of which foreign speakers are capable

(2)   *I am here since two years.*

must also explicitly prevent the production of sentences that neither natives nor foreigners would probably ever be in danger of forming, these sentences themselves being of at least two further types:

(3)   *Little a boy the ran street up.*
(4)   *Colourless green ideas sleep furiously.*

Already at this point the categorial difficulty becomes acute. That is, while no one would deny that a description of English must explicitly exclude (3) and (4) and that the native speaker has no difficulty in placing both (3) and (4) comfortably beyond the pale of acceptable sentences, plenty are ready to deny that 'grammar' is involved in excluding both of them. Nor would this seem to be a trivial matter of the traditional way in which the word 'grammar' has been used either in linguistics or in popular (for example, educational) practice – even if the latter could reasonably or safely be dismissed as trivial. The ability to see (4) as in some important ways perfectly grammatical (and differing from ordinary sentences only in being concerned with nothing that anyone would want to say) is matched by the reluctance to see its deviance as attributable to ungrammatical usage and by a preference instead to regard it as merely 'ontological nonsense' (cf. Bolinger, 1961, 371). Attention has been drawn to the fact that a 'distinguished philosopher maintains that "He had a green thought" is grammatical but nonsensical' (Ziff, 1964, 210), and it seems relevant to point out that such widespread reactions as those of the distinguished philosopher coincide significantly with the fact that there is little evidence that the philological tradition of any language brings deviations of the type found in sentence (4) within a grammatical description. (See further, pp. 65f.)

In discussing the question, however, in terms of 'the native speaker' and what he may regard as 'acceptable sentences', we are already encountering a new problem: the relation to be postulated between 'grammaticalness' and 'acceptability'. According to a recent statement by Chomsky (1965, 11) 'Acceptability is a concept that belongs to the study of performance, whereas grammaticalness belongs to the study of competence'. While there can be little doubt that there is something called 'competence' which underlies but has by no means a necessary one-for-one correspondence with 'performance', there must remain a very great deal of doubt as to whether it is accessible to experimental investigation. We would hope, however, that light can be thrown on this deeper faculty by the study of performance (cf. the implications of 'rectifiability', pp. 65f.; the independence of 'lexical congruity', p. 100), and at any rate it is with performance, via acceptability, that we shall be concerned in the present study.

While the magnitude of the distinction between (3) and (4) crucially affects the testing of native reaction (since, for instance, any direct question to informants will introduce an unmeasurable variable at this point if it involves the label 'grammatical'), it need not affect a preliminary categorisation of linguistic deviance as such. For the present, therefore, we shall not exclude from our sphere of interest any of the types of deviation from normal English represented by (1), (2), (3), and (4). But to these we need to add one further type. The four so far distinguished have one notable feature in common: they are readily and widely recognisable as 'deviant' by native speakers. The problem of grammaticality extends further than this, however, and there is a category of very great interest in sentences which – perhaps through relative rarity or relative complexity – are less readily assigned deviant status; for example,

(5)   *For anyone to have walked out would not
            have surprised me.*

We propose now to postpone further discussion of the categorial question until later in this study, since – as Ziff has said – it is necessary 'to leave the prim path of rosy speculation and muck about with the data' (1964, 214).

We may therefore turn to the second of the difficulties mentioned – the problem of how to estimate native reaction to linguistic deviance. It will be clear from the preceding paragraph that we cannot consider a direct question of the kind used by Maclay and Sleator, 'Do these words form a GRAMMATICAL English sentence?', or even – provisionally granting their wise suggestion that it would be well to provide for gradience – the form of question that they think 'might be more reasonable to ask', namely, 'Which of these two sequences is more grammatical?' (1960, 276, 281). Even if naive informants were not 'almost extinct', no direct question about grammaticalness could be addressed to them since this concept involves considerable sophistication, the situation being further complicated by the fact that there is no knowing what degree or what kind of sophistication. That is, we know next to nothing of what a given informant means when he says 'This is grammatical'. The point can be illustrated from several recently published investigations of the problem, but from none more dramatically than the little experiment reported by A. A. Hill. Of three informants who rejected *I never heard a green horse smoke a dozen oranges* as ungrammatical, we are told that 'two changed their votes when it was pointed out that the sentence was strictly true' (Hill, 1961, 3). When the notion of what is grammatical is confounded with eternal verities, it is time to look for other techniques of investigation.

One such technique is the direct question which seeks to steer between the scylla and charybdis of 'grammatical' and 'nonsensical' (or 'untrue') by means of a neutral formulation such as 'natural and normal language'. That is to say, although it may be doubted whether a group of informants will be able to distinguish with any reasonable degree of consistency between the three types of category implied by the key words 'grammatical', 'meaningful', and 'ordinary' in the three sets of questions posed by Maclay and Sleator (1960, 276), a formula is conceivable that can evenly and equally embrace the chief types of deviation. We have carried out direct informant-reaction tests on these lines, experimenting with a two-, three-, and five-point scale of permitted responses. The *yes/no* or 'excluded mean' type of choice is least appropriate since it acutely enforces an arbitrary polarisation in many cases, and we have had greatest success with a three-point scale, the additional permitted answer being explained to informants as a perfectly valid median or 'doubtful' reaction. Such a three-point scale is used in Zimmer, 1964, 95ff. By this means, results from a group of informants readily show the degree to which the *yes/no* distinction is clear-cut, since the more clear-cut it is, the fewer query-responses there are (cf. Fig. 9, p. 52). One also has a check on the efficacy or comprehensibility of a particular test sentence, since a high level of both 'yes' and 'no' answers with a very low level of queries would suggest that the test was ambiguous.

In most of our own tentative sorties in this field over the past few years, however, we have taken it as axiomatic that direct questioning is the least reliable technique, and that the informant's focus of attention should be systematically shifted away from the investigator's problem, as a necessary condition of achieving a controlled and natural (if not naive) reaction. We have experimented with the use of examination papers containing the conventional questions which require comments on sentences with various kinds of ill-formedness, and we have found that if a sentence contained one common deviation (let us say, a 'dangling' participle), this would be duly noticed and dutifully condemned, but that if a sentence contained a 'dangling' participle and in addition a 'split infinitive', an informant might notice and condemn only the latter. We have attempted (as part of an inquiry into the language of traditional verse) to estimate the acceptability and comprehensibility of unusual word-orders by eliciting paraphrases of such sentences as

(a)   *And every winding of the way*
        The echo shall prolong.

(b)   *His chariots of wrath*
                The deep thunder-clouds form.
(c)   *And all the air a solemn stillness holds.*

At the same time we required the same informants to fill with 'suitable' nouns the blanks in similar sequences like

(d)   *– – – – his mighty – – – – obeyed.*
(e)   *Many – – – – to my house your – – – – supplied.*

A further check on the informants' dependence on particular lexical items or classes of lexical items was sought by requiring them to label the nonsense noun-words as 'subject' and 'object' in sequences like

(f)   *Whose kon those little pippers rand which*
                now his nids envale.

In one limited area of divided usage, we experimented with an examination in translation from Old English as a means of uniformly estimating the usage of a group of informants with their focus of interest successfully shifted from the question at issue (Quirk and Duckworth, 1961). The translation of a passage containing some instances of the Old English negative preterite of *durran* produced a sharply different scatter of forms from that obtainable as a result of a direct elicitation, though the instances of *durst* in the 1961 experiment (14 in a total of 165) as compared with none in the experiment reported in the present paper (p. 90) indicate a defect in the technique through the obvious skewing effect of the Old English form *dorste* with which the informants were confronted.

While translation, therefore, proved a useful approach in successfully diverting the informants' focus of interest from the object of the test, and indeed in disguising this object, it brought in undesirable distorting features. In designing the procedure used in the present experiment, we naturally sought to avoid the disadvantages while retaining the advantages so far achieved. But there were further advantages that we felt it necessary to incorporate. Specifically, we wished to have a technique that would transcend the dangers of informants improving their performance by habituation in the course of the test, as in the experiment reported by Miller and Isard (1963; see especially p. 224). Equally, while requiring a method that provided a reasonable wealth of data, we insisted that it must not fatigue the informants by reason of either excessive duration or monotony of form. Fatigue is, of course, particularly liable to invalidate the direct-question type of inquiry, where, after exercising their judgment on acceptability a few times with some confidence, informants commonly complain (or reveal) that their feeling for such distinctions is seriously impaired.

Our way of achieving these objectives was to present informants with sentences on which they were required to carry out one of several operations which must be easy both to understand and to perform. An example would be to replace the subject *he* by *they*, and it would be left to informants to make any consequential changes that then seemed necessary. In order to focus the informants' attention on the operation rather than on the form or content of the sentences (and hence in order to disguise the real object of investigation), the test battery would begin by presenting sentences which seemed to pose no problem of acceptability, and it would indeed include a fairly large number of such sentences. So far as the disguise is concerned, we can at the outset report complete success: informants were questioned afterwards on what they thought had been involved, and although answers included 'spelling', 'handwriting', 'general intelligence', no one came closer to the point than this. Our measure of reaction to linguistic deviance would thus be the degree of success achieved and the kinds of error made in performing the operation, since if the informants were able to carry out a given operation on some sentences but failed on others, the difference could be attributed only to the degree or kind of difficulty presented by the sentences.

There are interesting points of comparison, therefore, with the procedure of Miller and Isard (1963) whose aim, however, was a perceptual inquiry and who took three degrees of acceptability

for granted as their starting point: 'If a listener's knowledge of
linguistic rules facilitates his perception of speech, one would
expect that ungrammatical strings, which violate both semantic
and syntactic rules, would be the most difficult to repeat, and that
grammatical sentences which obey both semantic and syntactic
rules would be the easiest. This expectation was borne out...'
(220-1). No doubt to maximise the contrast in results, Miller and
Isard took as their three degrees rather grossly divergent types
of strings, the only two deviant types, 'anomalous' and 'ungrammatical', being those corresponding to our (4) and (3) above:

Grammatical: *Gadgets simplify work around the
house.*

Anomalous: *Hunters simplify motorists across the
hive.*

Ungrammatical: *Between gadgets highways passengers
the steal.*

As these examples suggest, the entire battery consisted of permu-
tations: five examples of ten sentence types comprised the basic
set of fifty grammatical sentences; the anomalous and ungrammatical sets repeated this five-times-ten series, merely permuting
the lexical or grammatical items. It is not perhaps surprising,
therefore, that, confronted with so much item-similarity and the
single task of repetition for 150 sentences, informants sharply
changed their pattern of results in the course of the test (*ib.*, 221):

	Per Cent Success Scores		
	Gram.	Anom.	Ungram.
First ten sentences	85.7	68.6	35.7
Last thirty sentences	91.5	82.7	62.1

When one reflects that only eight informants took part in the test
and that doubtful aspects of experiment-design included the listing
among the anomalous sentences of *Colorless yellow ideas sleep
furiously* (closely echoing one which is now virtually a proverb),

one is left with some reservations on the Miller and Isard procedure. Nevertheless, the results of their interesting experiment are unambiguous and valuable: 'grammatically acceptable but semantically anomalous sentences are intermediate in difficulty, falling below the normal sentences but above the ungrammatical strings in terms of the measures of perceptual accuracy that we have employed' (224). In other words, degrees of perceptibility (equated with degrees of reliability in repetition) are correlatable with degrees of linguistic deviance.

We would like to assume the demonstration of this correlation in reporting our own work. At the same time, since mere ability to repeat may indicate only a superficial perception, we would prefer to take as the test an ability to perceive the structure of a sentence sufficiently well to perform a grammatical operation on it. Moreover, as already explained, we preferred a test involving operation rather than mere replication, in order to disperse the informants' attention and to avoid a technique that displayed a learnable pattern.

2

TEST DESIGN

Our tests were presented orally and, in many ways, we would have preferred informant responses to be oral also. Some preliminary experimentation showed, however, that the disadvantages outweighed the advantages: not only would scoring and timing control have been complicated in several (possibly trivial) respects with oral as opposed to written responses, but – crucially – it would not then have been feasible, without an unrealistic demand on time or special equipment or both (but see p. 104), to apply the test to a fairly large number of informants. Having established that variability of success rather than variation in time taken to respond would give an adequate range of results, our first tentative experiments culminated in a pilot application of a test battery consisting of fifty sentences to a group of twenty-five students, who had to perform a linguistic operation on each sentence. This OPERATION TEST confirmed that presentation of the sentences at twenty-second intervals allowed enough time for the majority of informants to complete the majority of the tasks, while not giving so much that there was an unrevealingly high success rate or time for informants to become unduly introspective (or to consult their neighbours). It also confirmed that fifty tasks at this rate showed no sign of fatiguing the students; that a single normal-tempo reading of the test-sentences was adequate; that we were introducing enough variation of sentence types and operation tasks (eight in all) to debar either learning or boredom; and that there were sufficient operation tasks, though it became apparent that some needed clearer and fuller initial explication. We found that it appeared to make no difference to ability in performance whether we announced the operation or the test-sentence first, but decided to continue to have both orders of presentation in the test technique to minimise the danger of habit becoming a factor. Above all, the wide variation in the degree of success in performing the operations, and at the same time the fact that the same sentences gave similar amounts and kinds of trouble to most informants, satisfied us that we were on the right lines in the experiment design.

Nevertheless, the pilot test showed that there were deficiencies too. The theory of our technique requires us to measure the kind and degree of deviance of the test-sentence by the kind and degree of accuracy with which the informant wrote down not the same sentence but the sentence changed in terms of a certain operation. The validity of our measurement therefore depends on each sentence having precisely the same degree of deviance after the operation has been performed as it had before. If, for example, the test sentence is

They /don't want some càke#

and the operation is 'Turn the sentence from negative to positive', a 100-per-cent success score would have no bearing on the informants' reaction to the original sentence, since in the correct written form of the changed sentence, *They want some cake*, no reason for disliking *some* remains. Some of the tests in the pilot experiment had inappropriate operations in this way. For example, in testing the acceptability of *I was sat opposite by a stranger*, we asked for the interrogative operation without realising that *Was I sat opposite by a stranger?* is more deviant than the original and for different reasons. Again, accidental skewing factors were found in one or two of the test sentences themselves. In testing reaction to the use of *very* as a modifier of past participles, for instance, we used the sentence *They aren't very liked*; many informants responded with (...) *very light*, the phonetic similarity making proof of the point at issue a little too easy to be interesting or indeed reliable.

In remedying these deficiencies, we decided to introduce two further dimensions in addition to the primary Operation Test so far discussed. In the first place, the desideratum of variety encouraged us to include tests directed to the elicitation of forms in divided usage of the kind that we had investigated in the previously mentioned experiment involving translation. For this purpose, the test sentence need not be in any way deviant, but as a result of carrying out an operation the informants would be confronted with a less clear-cut situation in which they had to make a selection from one of two or more possible forms. In these SELECTION TESTS, of which the operation thus remained an essential part, it would not be appropriate to consider scoring on the basis of 'accuracy' in carrying out the operation; our interest would lie in the particular form selected by each informant. For example, the question of concord when two co-ordinate subjects present a conflict of choice could be investigated by means of the test sentence, *Neither he nor I knew the answer*, together with the operation task, 'Turn the verb of the sentence into the present tense'.

The second addition was to include a JUDGMENT TEST in the form of a direct question approach to the same group of informants. A threefold choice of reaction was to be explained to them and they were to register their responses as 'Yes', 'No', and '?' according as the test sentences seemed to them to be respectively 'natural and normal', 'unnatural or abnormal', or 'intermediate between these extremes'. The set of sentences used in the Operation Test would then be read out again, at the same speed and with the same conversational delivery, but this time at five-second intervals. Since the Judgment Test results have been intended for comparison and correlation with the results of the Operation Tests, the decision to include judgments implies no retraction of what has been said above in adverse criticism of the direct approach. Moreover, since the Operation Test as a whole always preceded the Judgment Test, there was no danger that an informant could approach the operation tasks with any awareness that he was expected to react to the normalcy or otherwise of the test sentences. There was no such built-in requirement, of course, that among the operation tests themselves we should observe a constant order. In fact, since some test items (such as Tests 1 and 26, 2 and 27, 3 and 28) were related, different – and possibly random – orders would have been preferable. As it was necessary both to have auditory stimuli and to conduct the experiment as a group test, this was not practicable. Related tests were, however, carefully distanced from each other, with variety as to whether a regular or a deviant form came first (where such a distinction could be made aprioristically), and we may assume (with some support from what is said below on the question of fatigue, habituation, and the control tests: p. 25) that no problem of transfer effects arose.

Finally, in the application of the full revised procedure, it was decided to use the tests on two groups of informants, all of them undergraduate university students of about twenty years of age. One group consisted of twenty-eight 'English Honours' students (referred to as Group I), the other of forty-eight geography students (Group II); none of these students had taken part in or had knowledge of the pilot experiment. Such a group as the latter was thought desirable in order that we might compare the performance of students having some acquaintance with linguistics with a group that would have been, by reason of their academic studies, securely insulated from recent discussions of grammaticality – a precaution, we would hasten to add, not rendered necessary by our including in the test sentences any such semi-institutionalised examples of deviance as 'colourless green ideas'.

Care was taken to ensure that the two groups comprised native English speakers. Sheets of paper numbered in pairs were handed round, two for each informant, who was asked to check that his sheets both had the same number. The students were told not to put their names on the paper but were asked to write at the top of one sheet the name of the county (or, in the case of the few Americans, the state) in which they had spent the greater part of their first fifteen years. (This regional information is of little interest for the use that has been made of the data in the present study but it has relevance for the detailed study of certain results: cf. pp. 93 ff.) Informants were told they would hear a series of sentences at regular brief intervals with instructions to perform an easy operation on each, and they were asked simply to write down the changed form of the sentence as speedily as possible. If, in a given case, the task was not complete when the next sentence was read out, it was to be at once abandoned and the new task duly attempted.

The eight operations were then explained and illustrated, special care being taken to use simple terminology maximally familiar from the school tradition of the English-speaking countries and congruent with that of lay discussion:

a) PRESENT (the abbreviation used in Table 1): 'Turn the verb of the sentence into the present tense'. For example, it was explained, *they ran* would become *they run.*

b) PAST: 'Turn the verb of the sentence into the past tense'. For example, *they are coming* would become *they were coming.* (Since the school tradition does not consistently label the aspectually marked forms, we treated either form when arising from an operation as 'successful'; that is, *ran* could become *run* or *are running,* and *are coming* could become *were coming* or *came.*)

c) NEGATIVE: 'Make the sentence negative in the usual way'. For example, *they ran* would become *they didn't run; they're enjoying it* would become *they aren't enjoying it.* (We accepted contracted or non-contracted forms and also such variants as *they're not enjoying it* as a fully successful performance of the operation.)

d) POSITIVE: 'Turn the sentence from negative to positive'. For example, *I don't like it* would become *I like it.*

e) PLURAL: 'Replace a given singular subject pronoun by a given plural subject pronoun'. In amplification, we explained that the operation 'Replace *he* by *they* in *he likes it*' would result in *they like it.*

f) SINGULAR: 'Replace a given plural subject pronoun by a given singular subject pronoun'. Again an explanation followed: if the operation was 'Replace *we* by *I* in *we are going*', the correct result would be *I am going.*

g) INVERSION QUESTION: 'Turn the sentence into a question beginning with a given form of the verb *to be*'. It was explained that if the sentence was *You are tired*, and the required operation was 'Make this a question beginning with *are*', the correct result would be *Are you tired?*

h) INVERSION QUESTION: 'Turn the sentence into a question beginning with a given form of the verb *to do*'. This too was amplified: if the sentence was *He likes it*, and the required operation was 'Make this a question beginning with *does*', the response would be *Does he like it?*

Even after this degree of simple explicitness (which experience in the pilot test had taught us was necessary), the informants were carefully asked if they all understood the eight operations and what they were required to do. The general procedure was then briefly recapitulated (emphasising especially that the sentences and the required operations would be read out once only), and the test began.

When the fiftieth twenty-second period had elapsed, informants were told to stop writing and to pass in the one sheet of paper on which they had worked. Having collected these but ensured that informants had still retained their second sheet of paper, we proceeded to explain the second part of the experiment. The three possible judgments were announced and written up on the board with the corresponding responses that the informants were to register:

Wholly natural and normal	– Yes
Marginal or dubious	– ?
Wholly unnatural and abnormal	– No

Informants were asked if they understood the distinctions, and were told that the sentences they had been working on would again be read out once only but this time at much shorter (five-second) intervals. They were asked to make a snap judgment in each case according to the threefold scheme that remained on the board as a reminder.

In Table 1, pp. 106ff., the fifty test sentences are listed in a prosodic transcription (using the conventions of Crystal and Quirk, 1964) broadly indicating the way in which they were presented. The left-hand columns of the table also itemise the operation required for each sentence and the order in which the parts of each test were presented to the informants ('os' indicating that the operation was first stipulated and that this was followed by the reading of the test *sentence*). The abbreviated labels for the operations as they are given in the table are for the most part transparently relatable to the spoken form of the instructions indicated as (a)-(h) above. The sole exception is perhaps 'inv(ersion) qu(estion)' which embraces (g) and (h) in a single formula; this, however, is easily interpreted as either (g) or (h) when reference is made to the respective test sentence. The remainder of the table presents the totals of the Judgment Test results (the columns headed '+' and '−' corresponding to the 'yes' and 'no' responses respectively) and the 'success' scores in the Operation Test (Pattern Set A, as explained with the whole scoring technique on pp. 38f.), further necessary details being given in Table 2; where the product of the operation was in fact a 'Selection', the results are given in Table 4.

It may not be out of place to stress the point that we use 'success' in this report always in the narrow sense of 'technical compliance in carrying out a given operation while retaining the text as originally devised and as given in Table 1'. Thus, required to make *He is silly and crying* into a question, an informant giving the response *Is he silly and crying?* would achieve 'success', while a response *Is he silly in crying?* would be a 'failure'. A failure response may, in other words, be a better-formed sentence than a success and indeed may result from imposing a well-formed structure upon substance that is in some important respect 'neutral'. We nevertheless speak of such a failure response as 'replacing' *and crying* by *in crying*, and the expressions 'mishearing' and 'rectifying' will also be used in this speaker-orientated sense, without prejudice to the interpretation that might be made of the phenomenon of hearer-structuring in the wider context of general linguistic or philosophical discussion.

As already explained (p. 15), the test sentences included a good number which could be regarded as *a priori* perfectly normal and acceptable; for example, numbers 1, 2, 4, 8. This was partly in order to provide variety and to prevent the informants from having their reactions distorted by confronting them with an unbroken set of deviant sequences. But it was essential in any case if we were to be assured that it was not the difficulty of the operations themselves that caused failures in performance. The normal sentences were thus to be a *control*, and care was taken to see that all eight operation types were tested out on these 'control' sentences. The near-universal ability to perform the operations (a)-(h) on non-deviant sentences may be seen from the results given for Test Numbers 13, 4, 28, 31, 20, 40, and 1 respectively. By contrast, one should consider the relatively low success rate for these same operations in Test Numbers 19, 21, 42, 32, 7, 45, 12, and 26 respectively.

The control sentences, with their predictably high results in both Operation Tests (success) and in Judgment Tests (acceptance) made it possible to check whether the results were being jeopardised by the informants becoming fatigued. If we consider six control tests in the first half of the battery (Tests 1, 2, 4, 8, 13, 20) and six in the second half (Tests 28, 31, 33, 37, 40, 46), being interspersed over virtually the entire time span, reference to Fig. 7, p. 36, will show that informants were able to maintain a high success rate throughout the Operation Test. Furthermore, if we consider the Judgment Test in respect of the same twelve test sentences, Fig. 7 reinforces the claim that informants did not suffer fatigue, since the high acceptance rates for these sentences (in contrast to adjacent ones) show that their power to discriminate remained unimpaired also.

The opposite danger, that the test might be unreliable through informants improving their performance as they became used to the procedure, would also seem to have been avoided, since we note that informants were able to gain a high level of operation success with the very first test sentence while in one near the end (Test 45) they scored one of the lowest levels of success recorded.

3

INFORMANT ACCURACY AND HOMOGENEITY

Since there are Operation Tests in which all informants are capable of complete success (for example, all in Group I for Tests 1 and 8; all in Group II for Tests 2 and 13; all members of both Groups for Test 40), and since there are Judgment Tests in which likewise there is complete agreement (everyone accepts Test 4; no one accepts Test 3), there is a broad indication of 'validity' or 'accuracy' on the part of individual informants. Such general informant accuracy is of course further indicated (as was their lack of fatigue; cf. p. 25 above) by the high success and acceptance scores for the control tests as a whole. Since, moreover, the results of the control tests give us evidence of repeated success, they constitute evidence also of informant reliability. We are still left, however, with considerable room for abnormal individual variation, and the results must be scrutinised to establish the extent of any such distorting factor. The two aspects of the results to be studied in this connexion are (a) failures in the Operation Test, and (b) minority answers in the Judgment Test.

By (a) we understand every instance of a result other than one in Pattern Set A of Table 2, and it seems obvious that each individual's total of such results provides a good index of his ability to perform the task relative to the other informants. In Figs. 1 and 2 (pp. 27f.) we display the failure totals, in order of most to least, for each informant in the two groups. In Group I (Fig. 1), it would appear that only one informant (number 20) had an exceptionally high number of failures, with four others (12, 13, 19, 11) who were somewhat exceptional in this respect; at the other extreme, one informant (number 2) was slightly exceptional in being particularly successful at performing the operations. In Group II (Fig. 2), two informants (numbers 3 and 15) had an

INFORMANT RELIABILITY: Group I
Ranged according to failure in operations (o) but compared with minority in judgments (.)

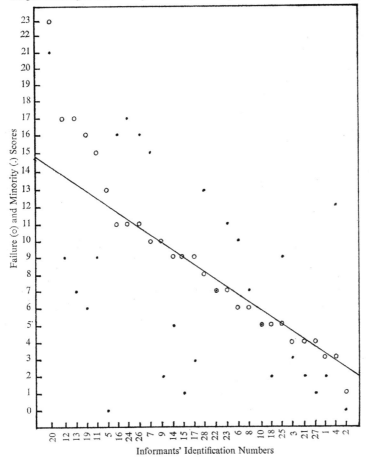

Fig. 1

exceptionally high number of failures, with one other (25) who was slightly exceptional in this respect; at the other extreme, two informants (10 and 17) were somewhat exceptional in their degree of success.

The aspect (b), minority answers in the Judgment Test, was rather more complicated to establish. It seemed reasonable to

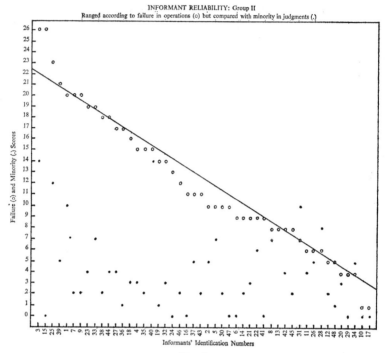

Fig. 2

ignore the question of minority when it occurred only in respect of the marginal differences: that is, between 'Yes' and '?', and between '?' and 'No'. Furthermore, it was equally reasonable to ignore 'minority' when there was a difference of only one or two between the acceptance and rejection totals (for example, 16 'Yes' and 15 'No') or when this difference was made insignificant by a total of queries that might be considerably larger than the acceptance or rejection totals (for example, 10 'No', 7 'Yes', 31 '?'). We decided to take account only of the difference between 'Yes' and 'No' totals, and then only if the ratio of 'Yes' and 'No' results was at least 1:2 and if the sum of these results was greater than the '?' results. Where results satisfied these conditions, we set up five minority-judgment classes according to the difference between the 'Yes' and 'No' totals: obviously, an informant who is alone in making a particular judgment would seem to be more erratic than one whose minority judgment is shared with seven or eight others. Taking the range from the sentences which produced near-unanimity in results to those with most evenly divided results, we made an exponential transformation to establish five reasonable groupings. A scale of weighted penalties was set up for each of these classes, and minority scores were assigned to each informant on the basis of the number of times he had appeared in any of the five classes; these scores are registered as period marks in Figs. 1 and 2.

These figures show that the range of informant accuracy in operation performance is matched only at the very extremes by the degree to which particular informants made minority judgments. Thus, in Fig. 1, informant 20 has both the highest failure and the highest minority score, while informant 2 has the lowest failure score and a minority score of zero; similarly, in Fig. 2, one of the two informants with the highest failure scores (number 3) is also one of the two with the highest minority scores, while the two who have the lowest failure scores (10 and 17) have no score indicating minority judgment. On the other hand, Figs. 1 and 2 suggest that there is in general little correlation between an individual informant's operation failure score and his minority judgment score. This is a source of reassurance about the quality of the informants' all-round accuracy. Thus, although Group I informant number 20 has a low success level in operations and is unorthodox in his judgments, the Group II informant number 15 who also has a low operation success level, has a compensating orthodoxy in his judgments. Similarly, in Group I, informant 5 has a minority judgment score of zero but an operation failure score as high as thirteen, whereas informant 4 has a low operation failure score but a high level of minority judgments. In Fig. 5 (p.32) the minority scores for the two groups are ranged from most to least, and it will be seen that the results for the majority of the informants show a similar distribution to that of the operation failures (Fig. 3, p. 30). In Group I only one informant (number 20, as we see from Fig. 1) is shown to have an exceptionally high minority score; in Group II

GROUP RELIABILITY: Failure in operations

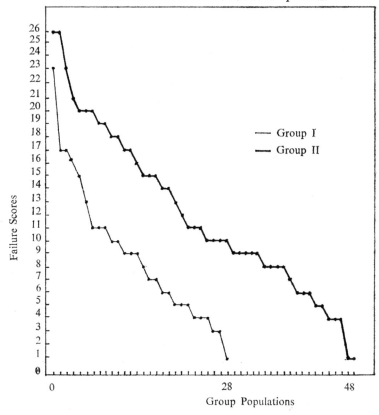

Fig. 3

five of the forty-eight informants could be regarded as somewhat exceptional in this way: in order of highest to lowest minority scores, they are informants 3, 40, 25, 1, 31 (see Fig. 2). It should be pointed out, however, that only three of these have a minority score of more than ten, whereas in the smaller Group I eight informants have a score of more than ten.

From the considerations (a) and (b), therefore, we may conclude that the informants are reasonably homogeneous both in operation performance and in judgment, and that the results of the test

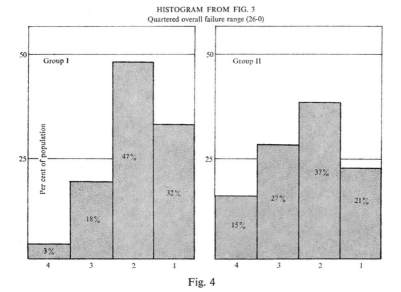

HISTOGRAM FROM FIG. 3
Quartered overall failure range (26-0)

Fig. 4

cannot be invalidated by the amount of individual variation that we have seen in the informants.

We must now consider the extent of any discrepancy in performance and judgment between Group I as a whole and Group II as a whole, and again it seems appropriate to do this in relation to failures in the Operation Test and minority reactions in the Judgment Test, both as already defined in the consideration of variation among individual informants. In Fig. 3, the range of failures can be seen, and it will be clear that the two groups present a very similar pattern in this respect: in both groups, near-perfection is very rare (one in Group I, two in Group II) and at the other extreme the worst performers reach a similar level (twenty-three failures in Group I, twenty-six in Group II), in both respects these differences being readily attributable to the fact that Group II is almost twice as large as the other. The only important difference between the two lies in the generally higher failure rate in Group II, clear enough no doubt from Fig. 3 but perhaps still more sharply brought out in Fig. 4, the histogram representing the data of Fig. 3. The reason for this discrepancy would seem to lie in the

GROUP RELIABILITY: Minority in judgments

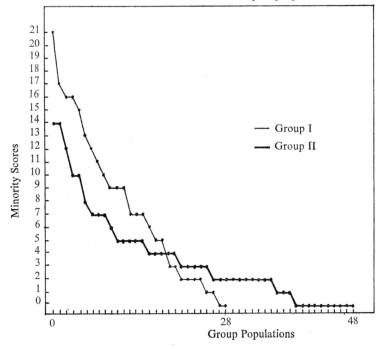

Fig. 5

consistently different academic backgrounds and interests of the two groups. The Group I informants, specialists in English studies (primarily English literature), are as a whole slightly more adept in the elementary degree of linguistic conceptualisation required to perform the operations, and are also – by reason of their reading and training – better able to control their skills even in respect of sentences which are ill-formed or meaningless. By contrast, the geography students constituting Group II have no experience of English studies (whether literary or linguistic) at university level and indeed have probably not studied English as an examination subject since the age of fifteen or sixteen. Since in this respect, however, the geography students are more representative of the educated community as a whole than are the students in Group I,

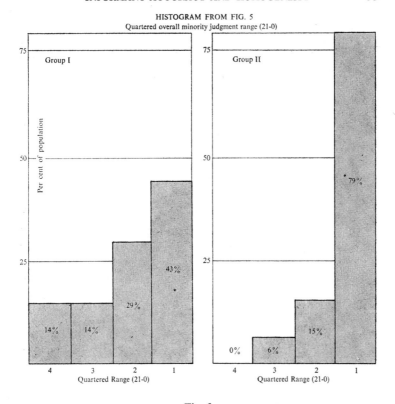

HISTOGRAM FROM FIG. 5
Quartered overall minority judgment range (21-0)

Fig. 6

the slight discrepancy in performance seems no reason for not conflating the results for the two groups.

To turn now to the minority judgments, it will be seen from Fig. 5 that there is again some similarity between the two groups: notably, the steeply dropping curves over the higher minority-score range. In the lower part of the graph, however, important differences appear: the Group I curve maintains its steepness and intersects the Group II curve which flattens out over the lower score range. In other words, far fewer proportionately (and even absolutely) of Group II are out of step with their fellows in recording their reactions to the test sentences (even down to the level of a minority score of seven), and this difference between the groups (which is sharply brought out in Fig. 6, the histogram representing the data of Fig. 5) no doubt once more reflects the different academic backgrounds. Thus, although we have found that the geographers are less adept in the operations, they are also more orthodox in their judgment of deviant strings, an interesting reflex of their not having specialised in English studies, being less attuned in consequence by their reading or general interests to deviant sequences (such as one finds in poetry) and less accustomed perhaps to making independent judgments in matters of linguistic usage. Since, as we have seen above, there is however a broad indication of agreement at the extremes (all informants accepting sentence 4, no one accepting sentence 3), we may conflate the two groups in respect of the Judgment Tests also, indeed in the confidence that by so doing we are achieving a somewhat more representative sample. From this point onwards, therefore, we shall in general refer to results as for a single group of seventy-six informants (for example, in Tables 2 and 3; cf. Figs. 9 and 7, pp. 52, 36), though for all the basic data the reader has access to the results obtained from the separate groups (Tables 1 and 4); Test 16 is a case where discrepancies make it desirable to look at the separate group results (cf. pp. 82f.).

4

THE OPERATION TEST

It will be seen from Fig. 7 that scores in the Operation Test ranged from seventy-six informants succeeding with Test 40 to only twenty-three informants succeeding with Test 26. On the basis of the various success-levels alone, certain groupings of tests suggest themselves and these are refined when additional evidence is taken into account. An examination of the different success-levels in relation to the number of tests for which each level was attained produced groups as follows: (i) 76-67, (ii) 63-55, and (iii) < 55. Objective as this grouping no doubt is, its adequacy is brought into doubt when reference is made to the Judgment Tests as well as to the Operation Tests. Since (following Miller and Isard, 1963) we assume throughout that acceptability is indirectly measurable by the degree of success in operation performance, we should expect a general correlation between the results of the Operation and Judgment Tests. As we shall show below (p. 70), the two sets of data have an overall correlation co-efficient of $r = 0.73$. The Judgment Test results (see Fig. 7) begin sharp fluctuations with Test 41, and a division at this point would give us a realistic grouping of the Operation Tests as follows:

(a) Tests 40, 1, 20, 2, 28, 23a, 4, 31, 8, 13, 30, 33, 37 (success scores 76-72);
(b) Tests 41, 34, 46, 38, 17, 9, 36 (success scores 72-67);
(c) Tests 6, 48b, 43, 11, 27, 14, 18, 49, 16, 15, 48a, 22, 39, 3 (success scores 63-55).

The group (a) would correspond to a minimum of 97% success in operation (accompanied by a minimum of 82% acceptance in the Judgment Test). There are two possible interpretations of the variation within this group: either the tests are so slightly

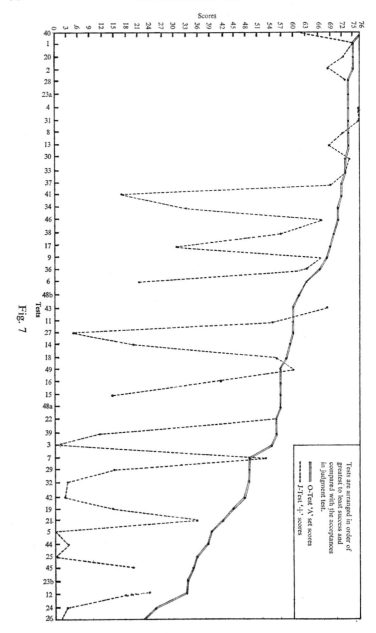

Fig. 7

difficult that any informant has an average chance of success of about 97%, or the tests are in fact without difficulty at all and it is only because of informant aberration that the success rate drops below 100%.

It is of interest to find that the tests thus grouped as (a) comprise all except one of the 'control' sentences introduced for the purposes discussed on p. 25 above. The exception is Test 6, *He isn't much loved,* which appears from both Operation Test and Judgment Test to be far less acceptable than we had realised when we designed the experiment. This should have become apparent in consequence of the pilot experiment when the corresponding sentence also had a low operation result. The sentence then read *He isn't much liked,* and since many of the failure responses had *light* for *liked,* we assumed that the problem was primarily an auditory one and we revised by simply replacing *liked* by *loved* both in this test and in Test 32 (cf. p. 19 above).

With the assurance that the high-success group (a) corresponds so closely to the control group of predictably acceptable sentences, we may take the downward curve of the Operation Test scores in Fig. 7 as corresponding in general to the decreasing acceptability of the other sentences in the test battery. But it must be emphasised that the success score alone gives only the grossest indication of the informants' reaction to a sentence and of the kind of deviance it manifests. A much more illuminating index of reaction is provided by close scrutiny of the failure responses. For example, the curve in Fig. 7 equates Tests 49 and 16 with a success score of fifty-seven. When we look at the informants' actual responses, however, we find that with Test 49 (*He pushed open the door*) those who do not achieve success failed through transposing *open* from prenominal to postnominal position, which apparently came more naturally to them; those who failed with Test 16, however (*Dusk was creeping up between the trees*), did so with a variety of errors: wrong operation, inserting an additional definite article, and above all 'replacing' (see p. 24) *dusk* by the presumably more congruous noun *dust.*

We therefore analysed the results, not merely distinguishing

total successes from failures, but distinguishing degrees of success
and kinds of failure. A starting-point in categorising the latter
is the fact that sentences in the battery deviated most obviously
in one of two ways, grammatically (including the usage of closed-
system words) or lexically: for example, Test 5 *John works there
either*, and Test 16 *Dusk was creeping up between the trees* (the
fact that the latter is based on a quotation from a recent 'well-
wrought' novel being, of course, beside the point). If an informant
fails in Test 5 with a response such as *Does John work there too?*, this
is regarded as a 'central' grammatical failure (that is, a failure at
the problem centre), categorised as Result Type I in Table 2; if
Test 16 has a response *Dust is creeping up between the trees*, this
is regarded as a 'central' lexical failure (again, a failure at the
problem centre), categorised as Result Type H in Table 2. Responses such as *John worked there either* (wrong operation) or
Dusk is creeping up between trees (omission of article) are classed
as Type G, 'peripheral' grammatical failures (that is, outside the
problem centre); *Does John live there either?* is Type F, a 'peripheral' lexical failure; ---- *is creeping up between the trees* is Type
K, a 'central' omission; *Does* ---- *work there either?* is Type J,
a 'peripheral' omission. Naturally, we find many combinations
of these types in the actual responses; a totally blank response
would for example be categorised as such a combination (that
is, as JK).

Between complete success and the types of failure so far discussed come intermediate features in the responses such as alterations and deletions, which may be taken as indicative of uncertainty and hesitation: these are Types B, C, D, and E in Table 2.
Type E indicates evidence of hesitation over a grammatical feature
at the problem centre; Type D indicates hesitation over a lexical
item at the problem centre; Type C hesitation over a peripheral
grammatical feature; and Type B hesitation over a peripheral
lexical item.

In setting up classes of result types and ordering them from
'nearest to' to 'furthest from' complete success, it seemed reasonable to class as Pattern Set A (i.e. general success) the responses

which included complete compliance, the successes with evidence
of hesitation (AB, AC, ACD, for example), and the responses
which gave two versions, one of Type A and one other, such as
Dusk (? The dusk) is creeping up between the trees (which would
be classed as AI). For the rest, we set up pattern sets on the basis
of a hierarchial interpretation of the failure types, which rated
F as less serious than G, G than H, H than I, I than J, and J than
K. The alphabetical ordering thus reflects the hierarchical ordering.
Pattern Set F, for example, embraces responses bearing type sym-
bols earlier in the alphabet (except, of course, Type A which represents complete compliance), but excludes those that imply a
more serious failure, so that Pattern Number 16 (CF) belongs in
Pattern Set F, but Number 23 (FG) does not. Similarly, Pattern
Set G will include Number 22 (BEG) but not 31 (FGH) which
belongs to Pattern Set H. In other words, each Pattern Set embraces the instances of one major type in relation to less serious
failure types, and the superordinate status of this type in each
set is indicated in Table 2 by registration as '×', as opposed to
'+', which is used for the subordinate types within the set. At
the end of Sets F, G, H, I, J in Tables 2 and 3, instances of the
relevant superordinate type occurring subordinately in subsequent
Sets are totalled in parentheses.

To sum up, the Result Types ordered from most to least successful are as shown in Fig. 8, p. 40.

On the basis of these Result Types it is possible to achieve a
more illuminating grouping of the tests than by the complete-
compliance scores alone, important as these undoubtedly are.
From Table 2, where the scores are given in detail for each test,
and perhaps more clearly from the summary of these data in
Table 3, there would appear to be primarily seven such groups.
Taken in the left-to-right order (corresponding broadly to the
gradient of success from most to least), the groups are as follows:

GROUP 1 (G + F, i.e. characterised by G- and F-type failures):
Tests 41, 9. There are few failures to comply with the instruction
to write down these sentences incorporating the required operation.
The other chief characteristic of the group is the evidence that

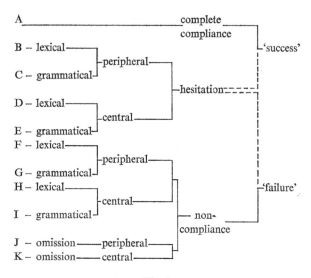

Fig. 8

informants cannot pinpoint their discomfort with the sentences, a discomfort which, as we shall see in discussing the Judgment Test results below, was acutely felt in the case of Test 41. In other words, there are no I-type failures, but only an odd peripheral lexical alteration and several peripheral grammatical ones: for example, in Test 9 some informants gave *He isn't what he pretends to be* instead of the required *He isn't, but he pretends to be.*

GROUP 2 (I + mix): Tests 17, 46, 34, 38, 36, 6, 48b, 14. The characteristic here is a low range of grammatical failures at the problem centre (Type I) and a slight scatter of other types. The rise of I-type scores throughout the group suggests – subject to important reservations – (a) a decline in acceptability, accompanied by (b) a widespread agreement as to where the problem lies. With Test 34, requiring *He isn't but he claims so* (compare Test 9 in the preceding group), some informants replaced *so* by *to be*. With Test 17, which required *The old man didn't choose his son a wife,* five informants introduced *for* with change of order: *a wife for his son*; with Test 14, however, involving another double-complement verb and requiring *They are regarded insane,* a larger number departed from the given form, nine informants introducing *as*, a further five replacing *insane* with *in saying*, and two replacing it with *the same*. These results would suggest that Test 17 is rather more acceptable than Test 14, and this is borne out by the Judgment Test (thirty-one informants accepting Test 17, twenty accepting Test 14), though it is worth noting that the 'regularisation' of Test 17 requires both insertion and change of order and that we might therefore expect more informants to carry out the rather easier regularisation for Test 14. Test 36 gives informants very little trouble on the whole but has a clearly defined central point at which emendation is possible for those who feel unable to give the required response, *Who do you want?* The only departures from this are the nine in Pattern Set I, all of them replacements of *who* by *whom*. Similarly, the failure responses for Test 6 (requiring *He is much loved*) all indicate awareness of the trouble centre, though in this case there is no such unanimity among the thirteen informants who give I-type responses, since no single obvious alteration presents itself: six gave *loved much*, three *greatly loved*, one *well loved*, another *very much loved*, and another simply *loved*.

GROUP 3 (G + I + mix): Tests 43, 18, 16. The characteristic of the group is a range of G-type and I-type results with some representation of other types. In other words, the test sentences give the informants some trouble without presenting a central grammatical point to which the informants' attention can be directed. One sentence in the group, Test 16, has however a lexical problem on which attention focussed, the required response being *Dusk is creeping up between the trees.* Fifteen informants replaced the abstract noun *dusk* by the concrete *dust*, producing a concentration of H-type answers (the highest H-score in the results), since auditory similarity presented an available alternative to *dusk* which presumably seemed more reasonable. The other sentences in the group, Tests 18 and 43, have perhaps a higher failure rate than might be expected when one compares the high acceptance score that both achieve in the Judgment Test. As presented, the sentences were *It's the man to whom I spoke* and *It's the girl I spoke to*. The high G results here (in fact the highest recorded) arise from a difficulty outside the problem centre (relative pronoun), a difficulty which appears only on performance of the operation, which would require *Is it the man to whom I spoke?* and *Is it the girl I spoke to?* There was a reaction against *it* as the subject in the interrogative form, and seven informants in Test 18 and four in Test 43 replaced *it* by *this*, while six informants in Test 18 and three in Test 43 replaced *it* by *that*. So far as I-type results are concerned, it is of interest to find more reaction against Test 43 (the more colloquial form) than against Test 18: three informants replaced *to whom* in the latter by $\emptyset$ + *to*, while in Test 43 seven replaced $\emptyset$ + *to* by *to* (or *with*) *whom*.

GROUP 4 (I + G + mix): Tests 15, 11, 27, 48a, 39, 49, 22, 3, 32, 42. This group is similar to the previous one except that here the I-type results are very much higher and predominate over the G-type; there is in addition a scatter of all other result types. Here, then, as we should expect from this array, are sentences which cause considerable resistance but which at the same time largely present a clearly identifiable central problem of a grammatical kind. For example, Test 11, requiring *Whom do you see?*, produced eleven instances of *who* replacing *whom* (a form over which three informants hesitated). In Test 22, the order of subjects *I ... he* was transposed to *he ... I* by seventeen informants. In Test 49, requiring *Did he push open the door?*, fifteen informants gave (...) *the door open*. Tests 39 and 42 also involve double-complement verbs, *choose* and *regard*, and the results should be compared with those for Tests 17 and 14 in Group 2 above. In Test 39, requiring *We regard him foolish*, thirteen informants inserted *as* before *foolish* (rather more than those who felt *as* necessary in the passive form in Test 14). The G element is important here, largely because five informants replaced *him* by *them*; this could be motivated by any of three factors: mishearing the unstressed pronoun, carrying the pluralisation operation over to the complement, or general confusion caused by the grammatical deviance of the sentence. The last is slightly more probable, since this alone could account for a further informant's replacing *him* by *her*. In Test 42, requiring *A wife wasn't chosen his son*, eleven informants inserted *for* before *his son*, where only five had taken the comparable step with the active sentence of Test 17, no doubt a function of the transposition that was additionally necessary in the latter, as noted above; one of the eleven informants converted the sentence to active as well as inserting *for*, and seven others also performed the voice conversion; other failures included three omissions of the verb and several wrong operations.

A further four tests in this group also involve voice, the first two concerning passive structures whose active analogues are of the form $V + prep + N$. Test 48a required (...) *were turned to* but produced a scatter of results of types G, K, and I; five informants omitted the verb, one replaced it by *attended*, five replaced *to* by *too*, and there were six wrong operations; no doubt this evident confusion was in part produced by the other half of the test sentence (48b, in Group 2 above). With Test 3, the first group of informants were required to respond with *Was I sat opposite by a stranger?*, but when it was thought that the artificiality of the first-person question form was interfering with the informants' reaction, a change was made and the second group of informants were required to give *I wasn't sat opposite by a stranger*; the sentence was of course constant in the Judgment Test for all informants, and it would appear from the rather similar results for the Operation Test that the change made no great difference. There was a concentration of I-type failures: thirteen informants replaced the passive by the active, only a few additionally transposing the nominal elements to give *A stranger sat opposite me*; four added *to* after *opposite*; two replaced *sat* by *set*, phonetic similarity providing auditory justification for avoiding the troublesome passive of *sit*. Test 32 required *They are very loved* and produced a similar pattern of alternatives to the analogous Test 6 (discussed in connexion with Group 2). Three informants merely omitted *very*, five expanded to *very much*, seven replaced *very* by *much* itself; alternative modifiers were *a lot*, *well*, and *greatly*. Other informants focussed upon *loved* and single informants replaced it by *lovely*, *loveable* and (curiously, in view of the trouble reported with this form in the pilot experiment) *liked*; while these might be said to have avoided the difficulty through lexical similarity, three did so through auditory similarity, replacing *loved* with *loud*. Test 15, requiring *Was food lacked by the children?*, might be described as partly grammatical (the rarity of *lack* in the passive) and partly lexical (the general stylistic and collocational restrictions on *lack*). Seven informants replaced *lacked* by *lacking* (followed by *by, for*, or *with*); one informant, elsewhere normal in his spelling, gave *laked*, while another produced an illegible word at this place; five gave *liked* and one *left*.

The remaining test in this group, Test 27, is predominantly lexical in the problem it poses, the required response being *Friendship disliked John*. No single solution presented itself to the informants, as can be seen from the scatter of result types; five informants stumbled in writing the word *friendship*, one actually wrote *fenship*, one made the word plural, six left a blank, and two attempted to re-order the nominal elements in the sentence. It is interesting that dissatisfaction with this 'meaningless' sentence finds an outlet in what seem to be irrelevant alterations which (if they are not merely confused errors through faulty perception or memory) cannot in fact achieve any improvement: six informants focussed attention on the verb, one giving *liked* instead of *disliked*, five replacing the bound negative morpheme by the *do + not* construction.

GROUP 5 (I high + G low): Tests 29, 7, 19, 44. The characteristic of this group is a small number of G-type failures with a rather heavy concentration of I-type responses amounting to more than half the A-type scores. The sentences are thus not only badly deviant but are deviant in respect of a grammatical feature on which informants can focus in perhaps trying to give a response that comes more naturally. Test 7 required *They are in the front of the station*; twenty-one informants responded with *in front of*, five with *at the front of*. Test 29 required *They didn't want some cake*; twenty-four informants replaced *some* with *any*, and several others showed obvious discomfort over *some*, with hesitations and deletions; one actually deleted *some* and substituted *any*, only to have a further change of mind, deleting *any* and substituting *some*. With Test 19, requiring *We provide the man a drink*, twenty-eight informants added *with* before *a drink*, and among other responses of minor interest, we find one informant transposing the complements and adding *for* before *the man*. Test 44 is the passive analogue of Test 19 and required the response *Some food is provided the man*; the results of the two tests, even as seen in the abstract of Table 3, are strikingly similar. Among the large number (thirty-five) of I-type failures, the commonest is the insertion of *for* before the final nominal group; this was done by nineteen informants (and a further two hesitated over such an insertion), whereas only one informant had introduced *for* in Test 19 where the insertion required nominal transposition in addition. In Test 44, on the other hand, six informants preferred to introduce *with* (the favourite and simplest emendation in Test 19), even though this entailed a far more radical reorganisation of the sentence: *The man is provided with some food*; curiously, one further informant carried out this reorganisation without introducing *with*. The results of both these tests invite comparison with those of Test 17 in Group 2 and Test 42 in Group 4, and we shall return to this question in Chapter 6 (pp. 71ff.).

GROUP 6 (I high + G + mix): Tests 21, 5, 25, 45, 12. The characteristics are a heavy concentration of I-type responses (similar to Group 5), a moderate concentration of G-type responses, and an admixture of the other types of failure, indicating, as compared with Group 5, greater general discomfort with the degree of deviance these sentences manifest, and somewhat less certainty as to how the deviance can be rectified. Test 25 required *A nice little car isn't had by me*. As well as the expectedly large concentration of I-type responses (twenty-three informants made the sentence active), we have the largest G-type concentration in the group, together with H, J, and K responses. The sentence was deviant enough for informants to be forced to leave blanks, replace the verb *have* by *hold* (twice), and even in several cases to write *A have a nice little car*.

With Test 21, requiring *I turned on the light for the room to look brighter*, the preferred structure represented among the large number of I-type responses was (...) *to make the room* (...), which was given by twenty-six informants, including four who took the further step of omitting *look*; one informant substituted *so* plus finite-verb clause. The scatter of other results bears witness to the general discomfort with the form of the test sentence: for example, two informants replaced *brighter* with *lighter*, one *room* with *look*, and one made no response at all.

Test 45 required *He is owning hundreds of acres*, and while twenty-five informants straightforwardly made the necessary adjustment by an I-type response (*owns*), many sought a lexical escape from the difficulty (only Test 16 has a greater number of H responses), replacing *owning* by an auditorily justifiable form: *loaning* (three), *holding* (two), *ruining*, *earning*, *roaming*, *loading*, and even the rather rare and technical *loaming*. There could scarcely be a more telling demonstration not merely of the unacceptability of *is owning* but of the lengths to which one can go in imposing either a congruous grammatical structure upon a given lexical sequence or a congruous lexical sequence upon a given grammatical structure. A further instance is however provided by Test 12, which required *Is he silly and crying?* The high concentration of I-type results shows that it was possible for informants to focus on the problem, but the admixture of other result types (particularly G) suggests that no easy normalisation of the sentence presented itself. This is very much confirmed when the I-type responses are examined. Most of them indicate an auditorily-based reorganisation: twenty-five informants wrote *silly in crying*, four *silly in trying*. Four presumably felt that the structure was more natural if it read *Is he being silly and crying?*, one if the uncomfortably co-ordinated *crying* were adverbially modified (*and still crying*), two if there were separation by a comma (*silly, and crying*), which probably corresponds to giving the sentence, if spoken, two intonation units. One kept the co-ordination but made an auditorily-justified lexical change (*kind* for *crying*). The B, C, E hesitations for this test (shown in Table 2) indicate discomfort also among those who in fact produced an A-set result, and one who did so felt moved to add the parenthetic protest 'Unnatural'.

Test 5, requiring *Does John work there either?*, produced not merely a large number of I-type responses but a larger number of failures in the K Pattern Set than any other test, these failures (as can be seen from Table 2) including a further six I-type responses. The commonest substitute for *either* was *as well* (seven), with five instances of *also*, three of *too*, and two of *neither*, while eight informants re-formed the sentence by simply omitting *either* (without leaving a blank); one informant, keeping strictly to the text, desperately tried to improve it by putting a comma before the last word.

GROUP 7 (I majority): Tests 23b, 24, 26. This final group is remarkable not only in having a considerably larger number of I-type results than the sum of the other types, but in having highly homogeneous I-type responses. These three sentences are thus sharply deviant, have deviance of a grammatical kind, and a grammatical deviance that invites a single obvious rectification. In the case of Test 23b, requiring *He turned to the Misses Smith*, the pluralisation of *Miss* was rejected by forty-two of the seventy-six informants and all sought an auditory escape, forty giving *Mrs*, two *Messrs*. With Test 24, requiring *Did they paint blue their door?*, fifty informants altered the order and gave (...) *their door blue*. With Test 26, requiring *Does he sit always there ?*, fifty-two informants altered the position of the adverb, almost all placing it immediately before *sit*.

More refined groupings could of course be made on the basis of the Operation Test results; for example, within Group 4, Tests 27, 48a, 3, 32, and 42 might form a sub-group by reason of their having caused informants to leave blanks in their responses. More interesting perhaps are the possible groupings that cut across those already established: for example, Tests 16 (in Group 3) and 45 (in Group 6) might be brought together as having seemed (compare the H scores) most susceptible to treatment as lexical problems, *dusk + creep* and *be-owning + acres*, since a good number of informants apparently considered the latter incompatibility more obvious than the grammatical one of *own* + *ing*-aspect. The detailed patterns in Table 2 suggest interesting cross-groupings too. For example, within Pattern Set A we have the similar scatter of hesitation results for Tests 14 and 39, the passive and active forms respectively of *regard* as a double-complement verb. Similarly, it is interesting to compare Tests 17 and 42, which have the highest level of C-type hesitations and which concern the active and passive of *choose* as a double-complement verb. But it would be wise to defer further groupings until we can take into account the Judgment Test results also, and until we are ready to consider the results in relation to a linguistic typology of the test sentences.

5

THE JUDGMENT TEST AND ITS RELATION TO
THE OPERATION TEST

By its nature, the Judgment Test is a rather weak measure of linguistic acceptability. In its most polarised form (acceptable/unacceptable) it is absurdly gross; in a graduated form (a seven-point scale, for instance) it is unduly arbitrary, since it is doubtful whether a given informant can maintain a steady grasp of the distinctions in the middle range between five and three. Moreover, in any form, its results are perilously difficult to evaluate, since in itself it provides no clue to the basis for any judgment. Nor, as we have insisted in Chapter 1 above, can the latter defect be remedied by directing the informants' attention to a specific basis, such as the extent to which a sentence is grammatical. With attention so directed, the informants in the experiment of Maclay and Sleator (1960, 277-8) made only a slight distinction between wholly unstructured strings of English words and utterances that one would have thought perfectly normal as response sequences. Thus

Label break to calmed about and.
and *A keeps changed very when.*

were acceptable to 14% of the informants, while

Not if I have anything to do with it.
and *Probably, although he may surprise us.*

were presumably regarded as little different, only 19% of the informants rating them as acceptable.

Nevertheless, the Judgment Test can be made useful if the grossness of the polarised form and the arbitrariness of the finely graded form are avoided by a three-point scale, provided a fine gradation can be introduced by conflating the judgments of a fairly large body of informants. And such a fine gradation is beyond doubt linguistically relevant. We do not follow Putnam in his belief in the all-or-none acceptability of sentences (1961, 40-1); he admits some exceptions but is 'more impressed by the multiplicity of non-exceptions' and by the general claim that native speakers can 'classify sentences as acceptable or unacceptable, deviant or non-deviant, *et cetera*, without reliance on extralinguistic contexts' (*ib.*, 39). As we have seen above in the Maclay and Sleator results, this need not even be true of what might be thought the grossly classifiable illustration that Putnam uses (*Mary goed home*); still less is it true of far more 'ordinary' English sentences. A selection of sentences with the corresponding Judgment results in our own experiment will demonstrate the point:

Test No.	Test Sentence	Yes	?	No
34	*They aren't, but they claim so.*	33	29	14
15	*Food was lacked by the children.*	15	29	32
17	*The old man chose his son a wife.*	31	24	21
6	*He isn't much loved.*	22	41	13

In three of these, there is only a slight preponderance of either acceptances or non-acceptances, while in the last there is actually a considerable preponderance of queries.

In fact, so far from there being a clear-cut line between acceptability and unacceptability, the collated responses of the seventy-six informants show that the fifty test sentences form a continuum with only two (Tests 4 and 31) being accepted by all and two (Tests 3 and 5) being accepted by none. We would however be dispensing with much valuable information, and would distort the results, if we based such a continuum solely on the acceptance scores (the thick line in Fig. 9) or solely on the rejection scores. The former basis would make it seem that Test 41, *Wood* (or *Timber*) *was creeping up the hill*, is held to be more acceptable (with seventeen acceptances) than Test 15, *Food was lacked by the children* (with fifteen acceptances), which would be mildly surprising; it is clearly relevant therefore to note that, whereas forty-nine informants rejected Test 41, only ten recording themselves as doubtful, a considerably smaller number (thirty-two) rejected Test 15, as many as twenty-nine being doubtful in this case. Similarly, this basis would virtually equate the acceptability of Test 6, *He isn't much loved* (twenty-two acceptances), and Test 45, *They are owning hundreds of acres* (twenty acceptances), and it is clearly relevant again to note that while thirty-one informants rejected the latter with twenty-five 'doubtfuls', only thirteen rejected the former with a very large number of informants (forty-one) taking up the intermediate position of doubt. The rejection and query scores thus once more supply crucial information on reaction to the sentences, but this does not mean that the rating would be any more informative if it were based on the rejection or, of course, on the query scores. A rejection-based continuum would virtually equate Tests 7 *It's in the front of the station* (four rejections), 43 *It's the girl I spoke to* (three rejections), and 28 *The woman sat opposite me* (two rejections), which have acceptance scores of 53, 68, and 73, providing a much clearer distinction between the three sentences and bringing the last two together in sharp contrast to Test 7.

In displaying the acceptability continuum, therefore, in Fig. 9 (which has the test numbers along the bottom in the rank order of 'most acceptable' to 'least acceptable'), we used all three types of response. We distributed the totals of query responses equally on either side of the zero line and plotted the totals of acceptance responses above the upper contour so formed, with the rejection totals below the lower contour. (The thick line represents acceptances alone, plotted from zero.) Other methods might have been used to distribute the query scores, but in view of the fact that there are, for instance, no results in which both acceptance and rejection scores are high but with a low query score (such as 36+, 0?, 40−), they would not have given a different distribution or ranking from what we have in Fig. 9. The figure illustrates vividly the gradations between the three types of responses throughout the tests and the absence of sharp dividing lines. It is of interest also to note the two peaks of query responses towards the right-hand side, representing reactions to the few sentences like Test 6 where there were actually more queries than other types of re-

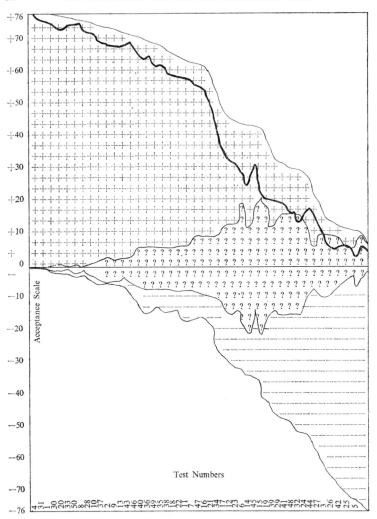

Fig. 9

sponse. We might also note that the incidence of queries and rejections tapers off far more thinly with the most acceptable sentences than does the incidence of queries and acceptances with the least acceptable ones.

In Fig. 10 the Judgment Test result for each test sentence is

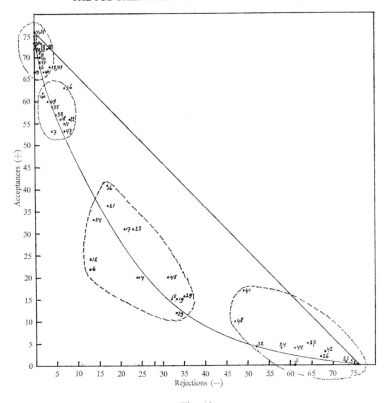

Fig. 10

plotted at the position determined by the number of acceptances (the vertical axis) and rejections (the horizontal axis) that each test sentence received. The dots are numbered to designate the test sentences, and on the whole they form a curve as shown. The distance from this curve to the diagonal between the extremities of each axis represents the proportion of query responses to the acceptance-rejection scores. This graph thus clearly endorses the point just made in relation to Fig. 9 about the typical 'query bulge' over the middle and lower range of acceptability.

While there are no very sharp divisions, it is clear from Fig. 10 that we can discuss the test sentences in terms of a fourfold grouping. The first group (to the top left of Fig. 10) has two sub-groups, the first of which contains Tests 4, 31, 1, 30, 50, 20, 33, 28, and 8, all of them – except 50, which is not scored for the Operation Test – coming within the group with the highest success scores in the Operation Test and thus very largely coinciding with the 'control' sentences as discussed at the beginning of Chapter 4. The other sub-group contains Tests 10, 37, 2, 13, 43, 9, and 46. These sentences are characterised by very high acceptance scores, with only sporadic query or rejection judgments.

The second group (towards the top left of Fig. 10) comprises Tests 36, 40, 49, 35, 38, 18, 22, 11, 7, and 47, at which point there is a wide gap in Fig. 10 corresponding to the sharp dip in the acceptance and rejection curves in Fig. 9. It is the largest group, and it is also the most typical in constituting an especially gentle gradation from sentences like Test 40 *Clothing was needed by the poor*, which apart from a small query score are generally acceptable (and which give correspondingly little trouble in the Operation Test), to sentences like Tests 11 *Whom did you see?*, 7 *It's in the front of the station*, and 47 *Neither he nor they know the answer*, which reach a query level of between fifteen and twenty, and have a sprinkling of rejections as well. It is a characteristic of the group that while the number of query scores increases steadily throughout, the number of rejections remains low, giving the impression in fact of being sporadic. In other words, the sentences are broadly speaking acceptable, but as one proceeds along the gradient in the group they give rise to an element of doubt by reason of their complexity (the correlation and co-ordination of Test 47, for example), minor deviance (as in Test 7), or divided usage (as in Tests 11 and 18).

The third group (in the middle of Fig. 10) contains Tests 16, 21, 34, 17, 23, 12, 6, 14, 45, 29, 15, 19, and 39. In Fig. 9, it is marked off on the right by the contraction of the curves bounding the query scores and by the slight dip marking the increase of minus scores. It has three notable characteristics: a much sharper gradient in Fig. 9 representing a decrease in the number of acceptances; a correlative and comparably sharp increase in the number of rejections as we proceed through the group; and thirdly a high level of query-responses. There is however little homogeneity, and in fact the second half of the group presents an important turning point in the test battery as a whole in having for the first time more rejections than other responses. Thus up to Test 6, the battery might be characterised as '+?', whereas the remainder are '−?'. The sentences in the present group range from those having rather little obvious deviance (such as Test 21, *I turn on the light for the room to look brighter*) to those that are very plainly deviant (such as Test 29, *They don't want some cake*). What homogeneity there is comes from the query scores, and the sentences may be fairly regarded on these grounds as the ones most acutely in the area where serial relationship (Quirk, 1965) is operating most weakly. We note in this connexion that both sentences with *regard* as a double-complement verb are in this group (Tests 14 and 39), and the active forms of *choose* and *provide* as double-complement verbs also (Tests 17 and 19), whereas the passive forms of the latter pair are in the 'least acceptable' group that follows; on the other hand, Test 21 with *for* + N_{inan} + *Inf* is here, while the analogue with the animate noun (Test 46) is in the first group above.

Finally, we have Tests 41, 48, 32, 24, 44, 27, 42, 26, 25, 3, and 5. These sentences are characterised by a small and sharply declining number of acceptances, a concomitant increase in the number of rejections, and a persistence of queries, reduced almost to the proportions they had in the second group (to which the present one shows some inverse similarity). Two sentences are included where the problem is lexical, Test 27 *Friendship dislikes John*, and Test 41 *Wood* (or *Timber*) *was creeping up the hill*, and three with seriously deviant grammatical features, two involving order (Test 24 *They painted blue their door*, and Test 26 *He sits always there*), one involving incongruous polarity (Test 5 *John works there either*). One is concerned with *very* + participle in a passive verbal group (Test 32), and the remainder are rejected passives whose corresponding active forms are in one or other of the higher-acceptance classes: Tests 3 *be* + *sat opposite by* + *N*, 25 *be* + *had by* + *N*, 48 *be* + *turned to*, and the two double-complement examples,

Tests 42 *be* + *chosen* + *N*, and 44 *be* + *provided* + *N*.

Earlier in the present chapter it was pointed out that the conventional direct-question test produced results that were difficult to evaluate because one could not know on what the judgments were based. In the present work, of course, the situation is different and the Judgment Test does not usually have this defect: it was introduced precisely because the basis on which judgments were made could be revealed by the Operation Test. The general way in which this may be possible is obvious enough. When we find that nearly a tenth of the informants fail to give the required form of Test 6 (*He is much loved*), we may suspect that the positive form of the sentence has given special trouble, but we have solid evidence in the results that it was the premodification of *loved* by *much* that informants sought to avoid (p. 41 above); when we subsequently find that even the given negative form of the sentence (*He isn't much loved*) is wholly acceptable to only twenty-two informants, it is not unduly rash to conclude that the widespread doubts concern the premodification by *much*. Other instances can be found where a conclusion can be drawn still more confidently: if we needed to wonder exactly why Test 24, *They painted blue their door*, is marked acceptable by no informant, the fifty informants who switched the order to *their door blue* in the course of performing the interrogative operation provide the answer. Nevertheless there are a few results from our experiment which show the persistent defect of the Judgment Test as a technique: Tests 13, 2, and 37 each have seven or eight non-acceptance scores which are inexplicable with reference to the Operation Test where (as we would expect *a priori*) the success scores were very high.

In any case, for the most part such general conclusions are by no means inevitable. Even in the case of Test 6, it is conceivable – however improbable – that the thirteen informants who made I-type alterations in performing the operation are among the twenty-two who found the original perfectly normal and acceptable. (As we shall see below, only three are in fact among this twenty-two). The results of the Operation Test and the results of the Judgment Test must be compared in detail before we can estimate the extent to which they can illuminate each other. In theory, there need be no relation between these results at all: half those rejecting a given sentence might perform a given operation on it perfectly successfully, and the situation might be that of the following table:

	Judgment Acceptance $(+)$	Judgment Rejection $(-)$	
Operation Success (A)	5	5	10
Operation Failure (F-K)	5	5	10
	10	10	20

On the other hand, it is theoretically possible that all and only those who succeed in the operation likewise give an acceptance judgment:

	$+$	$-$	
A	10	0	10
F-K	0	10	10
	10	10	20

Whereas in the former situation we would have demonstrable total absence of association ($r = 0$), in the latter we should have perfect positive association ($r = 1$).

To take as an example the data for Test 6 already discussed, correlation of the four types of result gives a table as follows:

	$+$	$-$	
A	19	9	28
F-K	3	4	7
	22	13	35

The probability of the distribution in this table is more than one in twenty (i.e. $p > .05$), but there is a slight tendency towards significance in that the ratio $19 : 9$ is inversely matched by $3 : 4$ (where a random distribution would lead us to expect $4 : 3$ or $5 : 2$ instead). It should be noted that, while the vertical marginal totals (22 and 13) correspond to the '$+$' and '$-$' totals for Test 6 in Table 1, the horizontal total for Success (28) bears no obvious relation to the corresponding total (63) in Table 1; the reason for this, of course, is that the query responses in the Judgment Test are here ignored and hence the Operation performance of informants giving such responses is ignored likewise. A still more accurate correlation of the results for each test sentence is achieved if account is taken of the query results in the Judgment Test, as we shall see below. A further refinement again would be possible if individual Pattern Set results in the Operation Test were taken into account.

In making the present limited type of comparison, we excluded the 'control' tests (which give an uninterestingly high success and acceptance rate) and the Selection Tests for which there are no Operation results. We are left with thirty-two tests whose Operation and Judgment results are related as in the 3 x 2 tables below, which indicate for each test the proportion of successful informants (Set A in Operation Test) among those accepting, querying, and rejecting a sentence $(+, ?, -$ in Judgment Test): A:+, A:?, A:—.

		+	?	—	Total	A:+	A:?	A:—
Test 3	A	0	12	43	55	—	.80	.70
	F-K	0	3	18	21			
	Total	0	15	61	76			
Test 5	A	0	1	39	40	—	1.00	.52
	F-K	0	0	36	36			
	Total	0	1	75	76			
Test 6	A	19	35	9	63	.86	.85	.69
	F-K	3	6	4	13			
	Total	22	41	13	76			
Test 7	A	37	11	1	49	.70	.57	.25
	F-K	16	8	3	27			
	Total	53	19	4	76			
Test 9	A	59	9	0	68	.88	1.00	—
	F-K	8	0	0	8			
	Total	67	9	0	76			

		+	?	−	Total	A:+	A:?	A:−
Test 11	A	40	13	7	60	.73	.93	1.00
	F-K	15	1	0	16			
	Total	55	14	7	76			
Test 12	A	7	18	9	34	.29	.46	.69
	F-K	17	21	4	42			
	Total	24	39	13	76			
Test 14	A	17	26	17	60	.85	.81	.71
	F-K	3	6	7	16			
	Total	20	32	24	76			
Test 15	A	11	26	20	57	.74	.90	.63
	F-K	4	3	12	19			
	Total	15	29	32	76			
Test 16	A	34	11	12	57	.83	.61	.70
	F-K	7	7	5	19			
	Total	41	18	17	76			
Test 17	A	30	24	15	69	.97	1.00	.71
	F-K	1	0	6	7			
	Total	31	24	21	76			
Test 18	A	43	12	3	58	.77	.86	.50
	F-K	13	2	3	18			
	Total	56	14	6	76			
Test 19	A	10	18	17	45	.67	.64	.51
	F-K	5	10	16	31			
	Total	15	28	33	76			
Test 21	A	23	13	6	42	.64	.57	.35
	F-K	13	10	11	34			
	Total	36	23	17	76			

		+	?	−	Total	A:+	A:?	A:−
Test 23b	A	20	8	6	34	.65	.36	.26
	F-K	11	14	17	42			
	Total	31	22	23	76			
Test 24	A	1	6	19	26	.25	.43	.33
	F-K	3	8	39	50			
	Total	4	14	58	76			
Test 25	A	1	2	33	36	1.00	1.00	.45
	F-K	0	0	40	40			
	Total	1	2	73	76			
Test 26	A	0	3	20	23	.00	.43	.30
	F-K	2	4	47	53			
	Total	2	7	67	76			
Test 27	A	4	6	50	60	.80	.86	.78
	F-K	1	1	14	16			
	Total	5	7	64	76			
Test 29	A	11	17	21	49	.69	.68	.60
	F-K	5	8	14	27			
	Total	16	25	35	76			
Test 32	A	0	18	31	49	.00	.90	.60
	F-K	4	2	21	27			
	Total	4	20	52	76			
Test 34	A	32	26	13	71	.97	.90	.93
	F-K	1	3	1	5			
	Total	33	29	14	76			
Test 36	A	58	4	5	67	.92	.67	.71
	F-K	5	2	2	9			
	Total	63	6	7	76			

		+	?	—	Total	A:+	A:?	A:—
Test 37	A	67	4	1	72	.97	.67	1.00
	F-K	2	2	0	4			
	Total	69	6	1	76			
Test 39	A	10	23	23	56	.83	.74	.70
	F-K	2	8	10	20			
	Total	12	31	33	76			
Test 41	A	16	9	47	72	.94	.90	.96
	F-K	1	1	2	4			
	Total	17	10	49	76			
Test 42	A	1	3	44	48	.33	.60	.65
	F-K	2	2	24	28			
	Total	3	5	68	76			
Test 43	A	58	1	1	60	.85	.20	.33
	F-K	10	4	2	16			
	Total	68	5	3	76			
Test 44	A	3	8	28	39	.75	.73	.46
	F-K	1	3	33	37			
	Total	4	11	61	76			
Test 45	A	9	13	13	35	.45	.52	.42
	F-K	11	12	18	41			
	Total	20	25	31	76			
Test 46	A	62	7	2	71	.92	1.00	1.00
	F-K	5	0	0	5			
	Total	67	7	2	76			
Test 49	A	49	8	0	57	.82	.62	.00
	F-K	11	5	3	19			
	Total	60	13	3	76			

It will be seen that, while A:— is the highest proportion of the three in only four cases, A:? is the highest in twelve cases, and A:+ in fifteen cases. In other words, with the latter there is positive association between judging a sentence as acceptable and being able or willing to comply with the operation instruction. Indeed, in three instances this association is so strong that, even disregarding the middle column of query scores, the distribution has a significance (demonstrable by means of 2 x 2 contingency tables: Finney *et al.*, 1963) of $p < .05$ (Test 17), $p = .05$ (Test 21), and $p = .01$ (Test 23b). Such association does not depend on a tendency of scores to agree – a high acceptance with a high success rate or a low acceptance with a low success rate. In Tests 6 and 17, as we see above, there is association between Operation and Judgment when the success and acceptance scores are in fact widely disparate. The associative tendency is present under similar conditions in Tests 14, 19, 29, 34, 39, 42, and 44.

There are twenty instances above in which the proportion A:+ is greater than A:— ; it happens that there are also twenty instances in which A:? is greater than A:—. The latter examples further attest the association between Operation and Judgment, since of course a query response indicates higher acceptability than a rejection response. Like acceptances, therefore, queries can be contrasted with rejections, and this is especially relevant when there are few acceptances or none at all. In Test 3, for example, the table shows that proportionately more of those who merely queried the sentence succeeded in the Operation than of those who rejected it. Here again, it should be noted, the association is independent of the wide disparity between the actual Operation and Judgment results.

On the other hand, in Tests 27 and 41, where the scores are similarly disparate, there is no evidence of any associative tendency between Operation and Judgment. There are important corresponding differences between these two and the tests showing the associative tendency. The latter include the sentences with the active and passive of *provide* (Tests 19, 44), of *regard* (Tests 14, 39), the passive of *choose* (Test 42) – the double-complement problems – and the remainder deal with the *much loved* sequence (Test 6), *so* as a pro-clause (Test 34), and negative + *some* (Test 29). All have in common a concentration of I-type responses in the Operation Test and within the I-type usually a concentration on one type of regularisation. By contrast, the tests (27 and 41) not displaying an associative tendency are ones in which the Operation results show no concentration on any one Pattern Set and in which the problem was lexical. It would thus seem that association between Operation and Judgment is greatest when there is a deviance which is attributable to a readily rectifiable defect, and one that is grammatical rather than lexical.

Before looking at an interesting consequence of this, we should examine the only notable instances that would seem to be counter-indicative, and it should first be noted that these are cases where there is no great disparity between the Operation successes and the Judgment acceptances. Test 16, which has *dusk* collocating with *creep*, is a 'lexical' problem in which nevertheless there is some evidence of positive association in the table above. When we study the detailed Operation results (cf. p. 41), we find – in Pattern Set H – precisely the kind of concentration of failure scores which we have seen to be a condition of Operation-Judgment association: the sentence was 'rectified' by replacing *dusk* with *dust*. Test 12, on the other hand, co-ordinating *silly* and *crying*, is also treated as having a rectifiable defect (twenty-five informants altered to *in crying* in responding to the Operation Test), yet so far from Operation and Judgment being associated by informants tending to fail if they reject, there is actually a tendency towards the converse association, as we see in the table. In both Tests 16 and 12, then, there are concentrations on a single type of rectification, in each case the replacement being auditorily motivated, and a similar margin between Operation successes and Judgment acceptances; yet in the first, despite a lexical problem, we have a positive association while in the other we have a tendency to a negative association. The reason for this difference, however, and for Test 12 being irregular as compared with the majority of the tests, is not hard to find. In the first place, far more informants successfully performed the operation with Test 16 (fifty-seven) than with Test 12 (thirty-four); the 'rectification' was thus far more obvious in the latter than in the former. Moreover, the rectification for Test 12 is a structural one (*SVC* to *SVCA*) that results in what would seem to be an entirely non-deviant sentence, whereas for Test 16 it is simply a lexical replacement leaving the basic structure unchanged (*SVA*) and the collocation improved only to the extent of having a concrete rather than an abstract noun as subject to *creep*. We need not be surprised, therefore, that the fifteen informants who showed sufficient dissatisfaction with *dusk* to make the perceptually plausible replacement with *dust* should be proportionately more highly represented among those rejecting the sentence. The situation with Test 12 is quite different, and we can readily conclude that the much larger number who substituted *in crying* did so because their reluctance to accept a deviant coordination was relieved by perceptually imposing an entirely non-deviant structure on the sentence which they naturally accepted in the subsequent Judgment Test. This would adequately account for their being less highly represented among the rejection scores than those who performed the operation without seeing a suitable rectification.

The remaining counter-instance, Test 11 (*Whom did you see ?*), produced a fairly high acceptance score (fifty-five) and a similarly high success score (sixty); there is a concentration of failure types, most replacing *whom* by *who*; yet none of the informants who fail is among the seven who reject the sentence as abnormal. It may be that there is no good linguistic explanation of this. Even where a particular association is generally expected, it would be by no means surprising in a set of fifty tests if there were some purely random deviations. Nevertheless, a linguistic reason may be postulated. We may have here a product of prescription-influenced judgment and perhaps of free variation. While *who* and *whom* are both perfectly familiar as object forms of the interrogative, some informants do not like *whom* (seven) or are doubtful about it (fourteen) and some – perhaps unconsciously – replace it by *who* in their own version of the question (eleven); but there is no reason why the seven should be included in the eleven. It is likely in fact that there is less consciousness of standards in one's own usage of such forms than there is in judging other people's.

These three tests which pose problems in the relation of Operation and Judgment do not therefore undermine the conclusion that positive association between the two for highly deviant sentences depends upon the rectifiability of the sentences. It is perfectly natural, indeed, that there should be such dependency. It is a matter of some interest (and perhaps not so obvious) that rectifiability should display a high degree of mutual exclusiveness with lexical deviation of the kind we have in Tests 27 and 41. Another facet of the lack of rectifiability in extreme lexical deviance is noted in an unpublished paper by our colleague Bernard Williams. He finds it significant (and the point has also been made by F. W. Householder) that such sequences as *Colourless green ideas sleep furiously* are fully and directly translatable into another language while maintaining a constant lexical deviance, and that in this respect they are sharply distinguished from sequences whose deviance is grammatical. Ziff (1964, 209f.) suggests that the degree to which one balks at a sentence 'could (in part anyway) be accounted for in terms of the degree of ungrammaticalness', and this in turn is directly related to the 'utility' of relevant linguistic categories. It is not very easy to grapple with a contention that depends on so charmingly informal a criterion as 'balking', but perhaps we may equate it with the query and rejection responses in our Judgment Test. Since by 'utility' Ziff means the extent to which a linguistic abstraction lacks 'ad hocness', linguistic categories having utility would seem to be those most readily available to native speakers (and least like those necessary to account for the deviance of Test 27 – 'animate-subject verbs'). In other words, it would seem that this concept can be related to what we have referred to above as 'rectifiability', measured by a concentration of alteration types in the Operation Test. If these interpretations are justifiable, our experiment gives no support to Ziff's suggestion. Tests 41 and 27, in which informants show very little ability to rectify, produce a high degree of 'balking' and – as is especially noteworthy – no evidence of association between those who balk and those who attempt to rectify. With Test 17, there is less 'balking' than with the two just discussed, but clear indication both from the concentration of rectification types and from the positive association of 'balkers' with 'rectifiers' that a rule accounting for the deviance is more readily available. In short, the careful conjunction of a Judgment Test with an Operation confirms the importance of Ziff's criterion concerning the availability of linguistic rules, but, unlike his argument, points in consequence rather to the polarisation of lexical (or semantic) deviance and grammatical deviance. As Katz has said (1964, 411), 'a theory of semi-sentences cannot be solely a syntactic theory but must contain a semantic component'.

6

LINGUISTIC GROUPING OF TEST SENTENCES

In the course of presenting and discussing the Operation and Judgment Tests, numerous references have been made to groupings of the tests in relation to similarities in test scores. We shall now look at the test sentences grouped in relation to the types of linguistic problem they manifest. Such groupings are of two types. There is a broad linguistic typology that will primarily determine the treatment here: voice, double-complement verbs, interrogative and relative pronouns, lexical congruence, and the like. Superimposed on this, however, will be a narrower grouping. With twenty-three linguistic sequences whose (obvious or putative) deviance was thought interesting enough for them to be included in the test battery, it was possible to match a further twenty-three in a one-for-one relationship differing only in respect of the deviant feature. The bulk of the battery thus consisted of paired sentences, the more deviant member of each pair being of course widely separated in the test sequence from its (obviously or putatively) less deviant analogue. The pairs constitute a basis for interesting comparison, and the discussion that follows will concentrate on the contrasting reactions to them by the informants. In the course of this discussion, reference should be made to Fig. 11 which sets out the Operation success scores for each pair in a left-to-right order according to the increasing difference between the scores. The test numbers are given at the foot of the graph, the respective success scores being on the graph, and the difference between the two being at the top of the graph for each pair. The differences were examined for statistical significance by relating the data to contingency tables (cf. Finney *et al.*, 1963, 2), and for all pairs after the first five (as indicated on the graph) there is a significance level of $p < .01$.

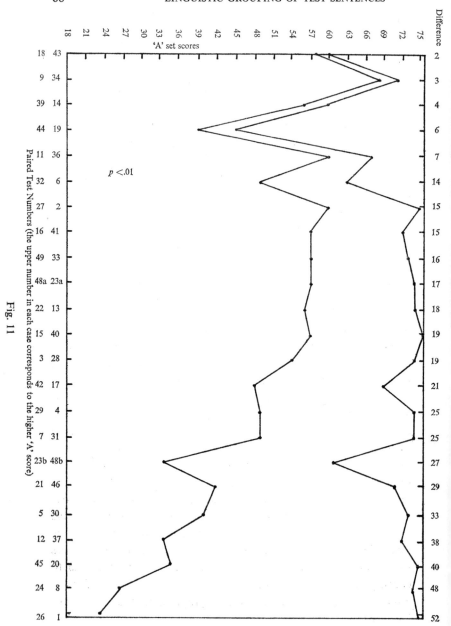

Fig. 11

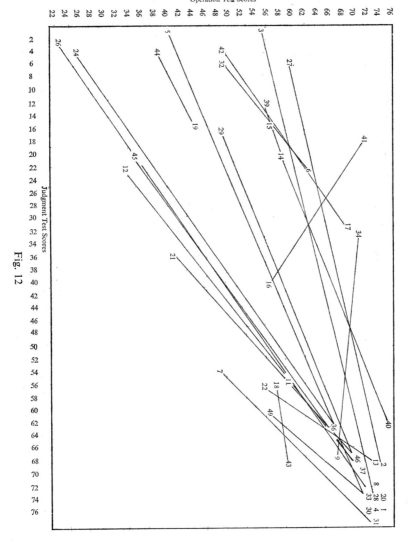

Fig. 12

We have already, at the beginning of Chapter 4, mentioned the degree of positive association between the Operation and Judgment Tests. This is apparent even from a casual examination of Fig. 7, p. 36. Despite the apparently chaotic plunges of the Judgment Test line, most of the points connected by this follow the Operation Test line reasonably closely, and even most of the plunges come down nearer to zero towards the right hand of the graph where the Operation Test line is likewise nearest to zero. The Judgment Test line is generally below the Operation Test line, crossing it on only six occasions. On the basis of these data alone (that is, taking merely the gross contrasts between successes and non-successes, acceptances and non-acceptances), it has been calculated that the Operation and Judgment results have in fact a rather high correlation co-efficient ($r = .73$, the 95% lower confidence limit being .48, $p < .05$).

Too much importance should not however be attributed to the evidence of correlation on this basis. The existence of the control tests (the leftmost thirteen in Fig. 7) plays a large part in producing the overall correlation co-efficient of $r = .73$, and if we were to disregard them, the correlation co-efficient would fall to $r = .5$. The scattergram (Fig. 12, plotting the same data as Fig. 7 but with lines connecting the linguistically related pairs to be discussed here) shows perhaps more clearly the variation in respect of Operation-Judgment correlation. The sentences whose connecting lines run broadly speaking from top right to bottom left are those which have mainly I-type failures in the Operation Test, whether this is a large I-type result (as in Test 26) or medium (as in Test 11). Those without this diagonal or radial orientation include the tests with a lexical problem (for example, Test 41), whose structure is clear enough to allow informants to perform the Operation with fair success while not presenting a sufficiently obvious way of rectifying a sequence which the Judgment Test shows they strongly dislike.

We shall begin by considering some problems concerning double-complement verbs. Two test pairs were used to investigate the relative acceptability of:

Test 33	*push N open*	Test 49	*push open N*
Test 8	*paint N blue*	Test 24	*paint blue N*

The sentences were so formed as to be of equal length, with N an identically structured nominal group within each pair, *blue* representing any member of the class of colour adjectives and *push* representing the small set of verbs (such as *leave*) collocating with *open* $+ N$. The results show the first member of each pair as having a high success score and a correspondingly high acceptance score; these sentences would seem, that is, to be fully grammatical. Not surprisingly, Test 24 is accepted by only four informants and flatly rejected by fifty-eight, achieving a matchingly low success score of twenty-six. As we see in Fig. 11, Tests 24 and 8 are thus more sharply polarised in acceptability than almost any other pair. What is less to be expected, perhaps, is the divergence between Tests 49 and 33 which, although not on the same scale as that between Tests 24 and 8, is nevertheless significant ($p < .01$) on the basis of the Operation results. These are endorsed by parallel (and in fact closely similar) results in the Judgment Test: seventy-three informants accept Test 33 and none reject it; only sixty accept Test 49 and three reject it. In both pairs, the member which is the less acceptable is the one in which the adjective complement comes between the verb and the noun complement.

Three further pairs examined reaction to another three verbs which occasionally appear with a double-complement construction; in these cases it was decided to test the construction in relation to the voice system:

Test 17	N^1 *choose* N^2 N^3	Test 42	N^3 *be* $+$ *chosen* N^2
Test 19	N^1 *provide* N^2 N^3	Test 44	N^3 *be* $+$ *provided* N^2
Test 39	N^1 *regard* N^2 *Adj*	Test 14	N^2 *be* $+$ *regarded Adj*

Again, undesirable variables were minimised by making the N elements with the same superscripts identical in structure within the pairs. Only one of the six sentences (Test 17) was sufficiently acceptable for informants to be willing or able to perform the operation on it with a fair degree of ease, the success score being sixty-nine; and even this degree of acceptability was scarcely endorsed by the Judgment Test in which it was accepted by only thirty-one informants, being rejected by twenty-one. We may note that in Fig. 12 the line connecting Tests 42 and 17 has a rather different orientation from those connecting the majority of pairs. Nevertheless in both Operation and Judgment, Test 17 is given a higher acceptability rating than any of the other five at present under discussion. In turn, the margin between the acceptability of Test 17 and its passive analogue is greater than between the members of either of the other pairs: Test 42 has an Operation success score of only forty-eight while in the Judgment Test it is accepted by only three, queried by only five, and rejected by sixty-eight informants. Thus for *choose* as double-complement verb, we find a fair degree of acceptability for the active but very little indeed for the passive.

The passive of *provide* in this structure (Test 44) is also rated very low: thirty-nine Operation successes, four Judgment acceptances and sixty-one rejections. In this case, however, the active analogue (Test 19) is not much better, with forty-five successes and fifteen acceptances. The somewhat higher acceptability manifests itself a little more strongly in the fairly large number of informants (twenty-eight) who give query responses in the Judgment Test and – as compared with Test 44 – the small number (thirty-three) who are prepared to reject it completely. On the basis of the Operation successes alone, the difference between active and passive here does not reach the significance level of $p = .01$, but if we take account of the evidence of the Judgment Test (in which the score difference has a high significance), the χ^2 test shows that the conjunction of the two sets of results reaches a significance level of $p < .01$. In other words, the active of *provide* is distinctly more acceptable than the passive.

When we consider Tests 39 and 14 (*regard*), there are interesting differences as compared with *choose* and *provide*. In the first place there is a considerably greater similarity in the acceptability of the two sentences: fifty-six informants are successful with the active form (Test 39), twelve accept it and thirty-three reject it;

sixty are successful with the passive form (Test 14), twenty accept it and twenty-four reject it; in each case about thirty informants give query responses. Secondly, what slight differences there are between the scores (much too small to reach a significance level of $p \leqslant .05$) would suggest that, if anything, the passive in this case is more acceptable than the active. To the extent that this is true, the reason may lie in the intensive relation between the double-complement elements (N^2 and *Adj*) in contrast with the extensive relation between the double-complement elements in the other two pairs; in this respect, the passive *He is regarded insane* shows serial relationship with equative clauses like *He seems foolish*.

Two pairs of tests examined the reaction to the active-passive contrast in relation to intransitive verbs followed by a preposition plus nominal group:

Test 23a N^1 *turn to* N^2 Test 48a N^2 *be + turned to*

Test 28 N^1 *sit opposite* N^2 Test 3 N^2 *be + sat opposite by* N^1

The N elements with the same superscripts are again identical in structure within the pairs. The active member of each pair seems to be fully acceptable: the Operation success score for both Tests 23a and 28 is seventy-four, and in the Judgment Test seventy-three informants accepted Test 28, only two rejecting it; there is no Judgment evidence for Test 23a, since there was the additional problem of the plural form, *the Misses Smith*, manifestly less acceptable as we see from the Operation Test 23b (thirty-four successes). Just as the active forms are similar in their high degree of acceptability, so are these forms similar in their margin of difference from their passive analogues in the Operation Test (Test 48a has fifty-seven successes, Test 3 has fifty-five), and this margin is wide enough to bring the results for both the pairs well below the significance level of $p < .01$, as we see in Fig. 11. In other words, both the above passive forms are significantly less acceptable than their active analogues so far as the Operation results can be taken as an index; and in the case of Test 3, they are supported conclusively by the Judgment Test where no informants accepted the passive of *sit opposite* and sixty-one rejected it; again no Judgment evidence is available for Test 48a.

The next pair contrasts *much* and *very* as modifiers of the participle in a passive verbal group:

Test 6   *N be much loved*   Test 32   *N be very loved*

Not surprisingly, Fig. 11 shows that the *very* modification is significantly less acceptable than the *much* modification on the basis of the Operation successes alone: Test 6 has sixty-three, Test 32 has forty-nine. It is conclusively endorsed by the Judgment Test acceptances (Test 6 has twenty-two, Test 32 has only four) and more especially by the rejections (thirteen and fifty-two respectively). What was perhaps less to be expected was the doubtful status of the *much* modification itself, as indicated by the rather low Operation success and Judgment acceptability scores, but above all by the preponderance of query responses (forty-one) in the Judgment Test. This unexpectedness corresponds to the fact that in Fig. 12 the line connecting Tests 32 and 6 is differently orientated from the majority.

Another pair contrasted the acceptability of the passive of *lack* with the passive of *need*, and we may also compare here Test 25:

Test 40 N^1 *be needed by* N^2 Test 15 N^1 *be lacked by* N^2

Test 25 N^1 *be had by* N^2

All informants were successful in the operation on Test 40, while only fifty-seven were successful with Test 15; this significant margin (Fig. 11) is endorsed by the Judgment Test in which sixty-two informants accepted the passive of *need*, only two rejecting it, while thirty-two informants rejected the passive of *lack*, only fifteen accepting it. The unacceptability of a passive form is even greater in the case of *have*: only thirty-six informants were successful in the operation for Test 25, while in the Judgment Test the sentence was accepted by only one informant and rejected by no less than seventy-three. An additional reason for this extreme reaction is doubtless the fact that the agent is expounded by a personal pronoun; the rarity of such an agent is discussed by Svartvik (1966).

In two pairs, we investigated the extent to which certain closed
system items are restricted to colligation with specific terms in
the polarity positive/negative:

Test 4 N^1 $V(pos)$ some N^2 Test 29 N^1 $V(neg)$ some N^2
Test 30 N^1 $V(pos)$ too   Test 5 N^1 $V(pos)$ either

The first member of each pair is almost universally acceptable
according to both Operation and Judgment results; Test 4 has
seventy-four successes and seventy-six acceptances; Test 30 has
seventy-three successes and seventy-four acceptances. The second
member of each pair is significantly less acceptable (Fig. 11) in
respect of the Operation results: Test 29 has forty-nine successes,
and Test 5 has forty; this margin is endorsed by the Judgment
Test in which only sixteen informants accepted Test 29 and none
at all accepted Test 5. On the other hand, negative + *some* seems
distinctly less deviant than positive + *either*; for the former (Test
29) there are twenty-five informants who were doubtful beside
thirty-five who rejected it; for the latter (Test 5) there is only one
query response while seventy-five informants rejected it. The
higher acceptability of Test 29 than Test 5 may be attributable
to the fact that there are conditions (for example, recapitulation
sentences like *He doesn't want some cake, he wants a lot*) in which
some can grammatically co-occur with a negative. It may be
relevant to note that its negative analogue *any* can similarly co-
occur with a positive, and that both *any* and *some* are grammatical
with both positive and negative questions: *Does/n't he want
any/some cake?* (cf. Bolinger, 1960, 380ff.). By contrast, *too* and
either are more sharply restricted to their respective polar environments.

An even sharper division between acceptable and unacceptable
(the sharpest that we found) appears to occur with the position,
among the sentence elements, of the class of temporal adverbs
represented by *always*:

Test 1 N *always* V A_{loc} Test 26 N V *always* A_{loc}

As usual, care was taken to ensure parity between the tests in respect of the N, V, A_{loc} exponents. The Test 1 order received a score of seventy-five successes in the Operation Test and in the Judgment Test alike; the extreme deviance of the order in Test 26 is indicated by the fact that only twenty-three Operation successes were scored and only two informants accepted it in the Judgment Test, with seven queries and sixty-seven outright rejections.

Two pairs which may be treated together, both by reason of their similarity in results and of the formal contrasts involved, are those concerned with personal interrogative and relative pronouns:

Test 11 *whom did S V ?*   Test 36 *who did S V ?*
Test 18 *(...N$_{pers}$) prep whom S V* Test 43 *(...N$_{pers}$) Ø$_{rel}$ S V prep*

In contrast to all the pairs we have examined so far, the present ones appear to have a closely similar degree of acceptability, producing extraordinarily even results not only as between members of the pairs and between the pairs themselves, but also between the Operation and Judgment Tests:

		Operation success	Judgment +	?	−
Tests	11	60	55	14	7
	36	67	63	6	7
Tests	18	58	56	14	6
	43	60	68	5	3

The results are especially similar in the case of Tests 11 and 18, the two sentences with the inflected *whom*; in each case, fourteen informants found the usage dubious and half a dozen rejected it. The closeness of the Operation success scores, however, is misleading since – as we see in Table 3 – Tests 11 and 18 are placed in different groups by reason of the G-type failure concentration in Test 18 (as in Test 43) and the I-type failure concentration in Test 11 (cf. the discussion in Ch. 4, pp. 42 f.). It is noteworthy that while eleven informants replace *whom* in Test 11 by the more colloquial *who*, only three replace *whom* in Test 18 by the colloquial 'zero' form with postposed *to*, and none at all by *who*. The implied tendency to prefer the inflected *whom* in relative clauses to the same form used interrogatively is given some slight support when we compare the Operation Test responses for the pairs. In the interrogative pair, *whom* is replaced by *who* eleven times, while *who* is replaced by *whom* nine times (Tests 11 and 36 respectively); in the relative pair, *whom* is replaced by zero three times, while zero is replaced by *whom* seven times (Tests 18 and 43 respectively). No such disparity of reaction, however, is suggested by the Judgment Test, in which the form without *whom* is in each case (and especially with the relative clause) rated considerably higher than the other. Thus despite the fact that in the Operation Test more informants replaced zero by *whom* than replaced *whom* by zero (suggesting a preference for *whom*), the Judgment Test shows a contrary preference for zero. This inconsistency, no doubt a product of the conflict between precept and usage, writing and speech, may explain the irregular direction of the line connecting Tests 18 and 43 in Fig. 12. If indeed the twelve G-type failures for Test 18 and the nine for Test 43 were disregarded, the line in Fig. 12 would be higher but would actually slope down to the right, thus enhancing the irregularity. The most obvious conclusion from these sets of results, and probably the most valid, is that we have divided usage with some doubts on the acceptability of either of the forms in common use.

There were several other pairs both of whose members seemed reasonably acceptable, though in these cases with sufficient difference in Operation and Judgment scores to make it perfectly clear which was the preferred form. One pair of tests examined coordination in which the first-person pronoun was one of the members:

Test 13 *he conj I*   Test 22 *I conj he*

The first of these showed its acceptability by a high Operation success score (seventy-four) in which no informant departed from the given order and also a high Judgment acceptance score (sixty-eight), with a few informants curiously enough expressing doubt or unwillingness to accept. With the other order in Test 22, fifty-six informants professed willingness to accept and the same number performed the operation successfully; in this case, however, eight rejected the sentence and twelve expressed doubt, while no fewer than eighteen informants departed from the given structure, seventeen replacing it by *he conj I*, one by *I do not ... nor does he*. In this connexion, we should note the Operation results of Test 38 where five informants replaced an *I conj my friend* order by *my friend conj I*. While the Judgment Test therefore shows no extreme dislike of the *I conj (...)* order, the numerous replacements of this (as compared with none of the *(...) conj I* order) demonstrate more clearly than the respective Judgment scores the preference for the latter order. There is a little further discussion of this socio-linguistic point on pp. 85f. below.

The disparity between Operation successes is greater in the next pair, while the more deviant member still has a fairly high score; the contrast here concerns complex prepositions of the form $prep^1 + N + prep^2$ which at one extreme preclude modification of the N and at the other extreme admit it fully. The forms used were:

Test 31 *in front of*   Test 7 *in the front of*

In the Judgment Test the first of these was given universal acceptance, and there was a comparably high Operation success score (seventy-four). With Test 7, there was an acceptance score of fifty-three and while only four informants were prepared to reject the sentence, nineteen queried it. This result is closely matched by the Operation Test in which forty-nine informants left *in the front of* unchanged while twenty-one replaced it by the form without article (*in front of*), a further five replacing it by a form of complex preposition in which the N remained modifiable as a result of changing $prep^1$: *at the front of* (cf. Quirk and Mulholland, 1964).

A disparity of a different kind is found with the pair which had as its object an examination of clausal abridgment and substitution:

Test 9 *They aren't, but they pretend to be.*
Test 34 *They aren't, but they claim so.*

Test 9 had a rather lower success rate (sixty-eight) than Test 34 (seventy-one), yet the latter had a far lower acceptance score (thirty-three) than the former (sixty-seven). The way in which this configuration of results is exceptional is indicated by the irregular slope of the line connecting these two test numbers in Fig. 12. As we see in Tables 2 and 3, the closeness of the success rates by no means indicates similarity in responses. Those who departed from the form of Test 9 (G-type failures) altered the sentence from a co-ordinated sequence to an embedded one of *SVC* structure (*They aren't what they pretend to be*), and no informant so much as hesitated over – let alone altered – the clause abridgment *to be.* On the other hand, the few who altered the form of Test 34 (I-type failures) mostly replaced the clausal substitute *so* by the abridgment *to be,* and one other hesitated over this, the form of the sentence as a whole causing seven informants to falter at various points. The scoring disparity is thus more apparent than real, and while one remains surprised at the large number who were successful with Test 34 as compared with the relatively small number who found it acceptable, the marginal status of *so* as compared with *to be* is amply demonstrated by both tests.

If, with the last pair, the Operation Test did not make it obvious which was the preferred form, no such doubt is left with the next pair, concerned with the plural of *Miss* + surname:

Test 48b *The Miss Browns* (...)
Test 23b (...) *the Misses Smith*

The latter, according to the *N.E.D.*, is 'regarded as grammatically the more proper'; this comment (1908) is repeated in editions of the *Shorter Oxford*, including the most recent (1964), but already in 1926 Fowler called it 'the old-fashioned plural', associated with formality and printed usage: 'elsewhere *the Miss Smiths* is now usual' (*Modern English Usage*, s.v. *Miss*). Current writers appear to endorse Fowler; for instance, Sir Ernest Gowers in the new edition of Fowler (1965), and in the United States, C. L. Barnhart in the *World Book Encyclopedia Dictionary* (Chicago, 1963). The Operation responses from our informants would certainly suggest little present-day familiarity with or acceptance of the *Misses Smith* type of plural, at any rate as a spoken form: only thirty-four informants replicated the form, ten of them with hesitation, while no fewer than forty replaced it by *Mrs*, and two by *Messrs*, despite the preceding article. On the other hand, the responses to Test 48b by no means suggest universal acceptability of the alternative plural, *the Miss Browns*; the total successes of sixty-one include thirteen hesitations, and among the fifteen failures, three informants leave a blank, three use an apostrophe, three singularise to *Miss Brown*, and six substitute the alternative plural, *Misses Brown*.

One pair of sentences sought to inquire into the restrictions on the form and use of adjuncts having the structure *for* + *N* + *V*:

Test 46 *I stop the car for the children to get out.*
Test 21 *I turn on the light for the room to look brighter.*

The first of these was replicated with a high degree of accuracy in the Operation Test, the success score being seventy-one, and the implied degree of acceptability was amply confirmed in the Judgment Test, in which sixty-seven informants approved the sentence and only two rejected it. With Test 21, there was a similar close agreement between the Operation and Judgment Test results, but in this instance indicating widespread dissatisfaction with the form of the sentence: only forty-two informants performed the Operation successfully and only thirty-six judged it as acceptable, seventeen rejecting it and twenty-three questioning it. In explaining the sharp difference in reaction, it seems highly relevant to note that the *for* + *N* + *V* structure as adjunct overlaps in function with the prepositional phrase, *for* + *N*, as adjunct; thus the relations present in *I worked for the children* are still present in *I worked for the children to be happy*, where of course there is additionally present the non-finite verb conversion of the equative clause, *the children* + *be* + *happy*. This, in part at least, is why sentences with *for* + *N* + *V* adjuncts are most acceptable where it is possible for the *for* + *N* part alone to operate as adjunct; hence, with Test 46, *I stop the car for the children*, but with Test 21, **I turn on the light for the room*. Clearly, the unacceptability of the latter is a function of *room* being an inanimate noun. It is important to stress that this is a question of adjunct sentence elements only; *I asked for the children to come* and *I asked for the room to look brighter* are probably both equally acceptable, since the non-finite verb clause in each case here is complement to the verbal phrase, *ask for*; we may compare *I wanted the children to come*; *I wanted the room to look brighter*. (See further: Svartvik, 1965.)

There are similar margins between the scores for the next pair of sentences which concern the dependence of co-ordination on the grammatical parity of the items co-ordinated:

Test 37   (*N be*) *clever and pretty*
Test 12   (*N be*) *silly and crying*

The first is given high scores in both tests: seventy-two successes and sixty-nine acceptances; the second has only thirty-four successes and twenty-four acceptances, thirteen informants rejecting it, the majority (thirty-nine) regarding it as dubious. As we have already seen in Ch. 4, p. 46, most of those who did not retain the co-ordination in Test 12 regularised the sentence by the auditorily explicable and structurally justifiable alteration from *and crying* to *in crying* or *in trying*, and several others displayed their unease with the given form by hesitation, inserting commas, and one made the lexico-grammatical replacement of *crying* by *kind*. Operation and Judgment results alike testify to the reluctance of informants to co-ordinate grammatically disparate items.

Again with similar margins between the scores, we have the pair of sentences concerned with the aspectual restriction on verbs of the class represented by *own*:

Test 20 N^1 *own* N^2 Test 45 N^1 *be owning* N^2

The first may be described as universally acceptable, an Operation success score of seventy-five being matched by a Judgment acceptance score of seventy-three, with no rejections. By contrast, Test 45 has only thirty-five Operation successes and twenty acceptances; thirty-one informants rejected it and twenty-five were dubious. Scrutiny of the Operation results shows that most of the informants who failed the Operation Test chose to make the grammatical rectification of *is owning* to *owns*, but (as we have seen above, p. 46) for a good many the solution seemed to lie in a lexical rectification. In either case, the results demonstrate the extreme unacceptability of *own* in what Twaddell (1963, 2) calls the 'limited duration' form of the verb.

With two pairs of sentences, we tested reaction to the situation in which lexical rectification would be virtually the only course open to informants. The first such pair was:

Test 2 *Jack admired sincerity.*
Test 27 *Friendship dislikes John.*

Test 2 presented no difficulty in the Operation Test (seventy-five successes) and sixty-eight informants accepted it in the Judgment Test, the only surprise being the seven who found it dubious and the one who rejected it. Test 27, however, was accepted by only five informants and rejected by sixty-four. This decisive verdict is glaringly unmatched by the Operation results in which as many as sixty informants performed the task without altering the form of the sentence. We should not conclude, however, that these sixty were tacitly approving the sentence; sixteen of them showed signs of hesitation, and as we have seen in Ch. 4 (p. 44), the wide scatter in the types of failure responses suggests that the high success score is largely due to there being no obvious or easy emendation. While such difficulty is by no means confined to lexical deviations (cf. Test 3), it would seem to be inherent in lexical deviations, as we see in the last pair of sentences to be discussed here:

Test 16 *Dusk was creeping up between the trees.*
Test 41 (Gp I) *Wood was creeping up the hill.*
         (Gp II) *Timber was creeping up the hill.*

It should be noted that these two tests were not chosen to compare the extremes of deviance and non-deviance as has been the case with the majority of the paired sentences. Rather, having encountered the collocation *dusk* + *creep* in a novel, we thought it would be interesting to have informant-reactions to it and to explore further collocates with *creep* as in Test 41. The Operation and Judgment Tests showed that informants in fact regarded both sentences as deviant, and hence the irregular orientation of the line connecting the test numbers in Fig. 12.

Like Test 27, Test 41 has a high Operation success score (seventy-two) in spite of the very low acceptance score of seventeen (forty-nine rejecting it outright). Again, it seems appropriate to explain the apparent discrepancy as due to the absence of any reasonable or available rectification. With Test 16, however, the situation is more complicated. There is both a lower success score and a higher acceptance score than for Test 41, the former suggesting less acceptability, the latter more. As we have seen in Ch. 5, pp. 63f., the lower Operation success score is attributable to there being available an auditorily-motivated replacement *dust* which – at any rate in being concrete – presumably seemed a more reasonable collocate for *creep* than *dusk*. One cannot know for certain how many of those accepting the sentence in the Judgment Test perceived it as having *dust*, but it seems reasonable to suppose that most of them were accepting the metaphorical *dusk* form, especially as seventy-five per cent of the English students (Group I informants) accepted the sentence as compared with forty-two per cent of the geography students – one of the very few serious discrepancies, indeed, between the two groups' reactions.

7

THE SELECTION TEST

As explained in Chapter 2, the test battery included problems of selection partly for the purpose of maximising variety in the test as a whole. Even if this motive had not existed, however, the inclusion of Selection Tests would still have been desirable, since a technique for eliciting forms in free variation is very much needed, and the operation procedure presents such a technique in a particularly convenient and efficient form. The principle as developed here is to confront informants with a sentence which as it stands presents no problem of selection, but which presents such a problem in consequence of carrying out a particular operation that the informant is instructed to perform. For example, with *Neither he nor I knew the answer*, no problem of concord arises; but, without having his attention specifically directed to it, the informant finds himself forced to make a concord choice when he is asked to convert it from past to present.

The tests involving selection on performance of an operation were numbers 13, 22, 47 (subject-verb concord); 38 (negative correlatives); 10 (negation of *dare*); 35 (of *need*); and 50 (of *have*). Like the last, Test 25 presented such a problem for the twenty-three informants who replaced the passive form of *have* by the active (I-type responses in Tables 2 and 3), and the selections made in consequence by these informants are scored as additional Selection Test results. A summary of all the selections is given in Table 4.

On the problem of subject-verb concord, Tests 13 and 22 should be taken together. There are three main concord problems involving disjunctive (exclusive) co-ordinate subjects: two singular nominal groups (as in *the man or the woman V*), where present tense enforces a choice between singular and plural verb; a singular and a plural nominal group, where again the verb requires a number choice; the first person singular pronoun and a singular nominal group, where person involves a choice of verb forms, though, apart from those of the verb *be*, the forms concerned coincide with the number choice. Tests 13 and 22 deal with the latter problem, though, since *be* imposes a unique range of choices, it was decided to generalise the test by having it apply to the open class verbs having only a marked (singular/third person) versus an unmarked form. Two tests were necessary in order to be able to assess the influence of order and in particular the influence of the subject-form immediately preceding the verb. With the tense operation correctly performed (as was done by all informants in Test 13, by all except one in Test 22), the sentences would have the following possible forms:

$$\text{Test 13} \quad \textit{Neither he nor I} \begin{Bmatrix} \textit{know} \\ \textit{knows} \end{Bmatrix} \textit{the answer.}$$

$$\text{Test 22} \quad \textit{Neither I nor he} \begin{Bmatrix} \textit{feel} \\ \textit{feels} \end{Bmatrix} \textit{a thing.}$$

There is a sociolinguistic complication with Test 22, however, because of the self-effacing convention of putting the first-person pronoun last; this produces a further basic choice:

$$\textit{Neither he nor I} \begin{Bmatrix} \textit{feel} \\ \textit{feels} \end{Bmatrix} \textit{a thing.}$$

The discomfort occasioned by the order given in the test can be assessed in Table 4 by the fact that sixteen informants adopted the switched order in Test 22 (while in Test 13 no informant departed from the given order, *he ... I*), and also by the rather drastic departure from the original by one informant: *I do not feel a thing – nor does he*. In this case, however, the motivation for change was no doubt partly the other cause for discomfort: the apparent feeling that neither of the obvious forms to be selected gave an acceptable English sentence. Certainly, only this can explain the similarly drastic step taken by the same informant in Test 13, where again separate concords are used for the two subjects: *Neither he knows nor I know the answer.* This would also seem to be the reason for one informant's introduction of commas in Test 22 (... *I, nor he, feel* ...) presumably in an attempt to make *nor he* merely parenthetic between the concordant forms *I* ... *feel.*

For the most part, however, discomfort over selection is expressed only in the evidence of hesitation (five informants in Test 13, ten in Test 22), and we have otherwise a straightforward division in the choice of forms. In Test 13, fifty-three informants selected the unmarked form, *know*, while twenty-two selected the marked form, *knows.* In Test 22, disregarding for a moment the variation in subject-order, we find a strikingly similar proportion: forty-nine informants selected the unmarked form and twenty-three the marked. In both tests, unmarked and marked forms are thus selected in the ratio of more than 2 : 1. Since in Test 13 this occurred with the universal order *he conj I* and in Test 22 it occurred with a majority order of *I conj he*, we may firmly conclude that the unmarked form is the preferred one regardless of the concord requirement of the particular subject immediately preceding the verb. On the other hand, closer inspection of the data shows that the tendency is somewhat smaller if the subject nearest to the verb is one that normally colligates with the marked form:

		Unmarked	Marked
Test 13	... *I V*	53	22
	... *he V*	—	—
Test 22	... *I V*	13	3
	... *he V*	36	20

We thus have *I* followed by the unmarked (that is, its concordant) form in the proportion 66 : 25, while *he* is followed by the unmarked form only in the proportion 36 : 20. When we reflect, however, that the latter means the selection of an immediately discordant form in the ratio of almost 2 : 1, we see that the strength of the tendency to select the unmarked form with disjunctive co-ordination is extremely powerful.

The results of Test 47 would seem, on the face of it, to be an even clearer endorsement of the rule. On performance of the operation the basic choice here is:

$$\left\{ \begin{array}{l} Do \\ Does \end{array} \right\} \text{ neither he nor they know the answer ?}$$

There would seem to be little motivation to change the order of subjects here, though in fact six informants make this change (and one other does so but abandons it), not presumably on socio-linguistic grounds but in order to bring concordant elements (*do* and *they*) together. Grouping and totalling the relevant results in Table 4 (ignoring, for example, those that have *either of them* instead of *he ... they*), we have fifty-nine instances of *do* and ten of *does*. Considered in relation to the nearest subject form, we have the following distribution:

	Unmarked	Marked
V he ...	54	10
V they ...	5	0

In view of the 54 : 5 ratio in the left column (that is, the rarity of subject-order change), we cannot regard the total absence of a discordant *does they* sequence as having any significance.

The high preponderance of the unmarked *do* in this test cannot easily or without hazard be related to the considerably slighter preference for the unmarked forms in Tests 13 and 22. In the first place, the interrogative order may well be an important factor in reducing the influence of a particular subject form on the selection of a verb form. A second factor, unfortunately, is likely to be more relevant: the form of the operation instruction (see p. 23 above) could hardly fail to bias the selection in favour of *do*. This is a defect in test design that would only in part be remedied by emending the instruction to 'Make this sentence a question introduced by a form of the verb *do*', since the generalised label (citation form) for the verb still coincides with one of the possible selection forms (and, doubtless, the preferred one). A better instruction perhaps would be 'Make this an inversion question' or even 'Make this a *yes/no* question', but either of these would involve a rather more detailed and sophisticated explanation period if one is to minimise null results through wrong operation (especially *wh*-questions) or through the informants having to spend too long puzzling out what they must do.

With Test 47, at any rate, we must treat its results with reserve so far as verb-form selection is concerned, however interesting they are in other respects. There is, for instance, the sporadic use of oblique forms of the subject pronouns: *do either him or they, do either him or them, does either him or they, do they or him* (this last with the oblique form subsequently deleted and *he* substituted). All of these occur among Group II informants, but, since they are much more numerous than Group I, we can hardly attribute this deviance to the difference in academic studies. The oblique forms are indeed too small in number to allow anything beyond speculation, but one may note that there are more instances of *him* than of *them*; that co-ordination is probably relevant (plus separation of the verb and subject, especially by the correlative element *either*), since Tests 1, 3, 12, 24, 26, 33, 37, and 49 all involved interrogative order with inflectable pronouns without a single oblique pronoun form being used; that nevertheless interrogative order is probably relevant also, since the analogous co-ordinated subjects in Tests 13, 22, 38 did not give rise to any use of oblique forms.

The other main interest of the Test 47 results lies in the imbalance that exists between the interrogative forms of positive and negative sentences. Since the inversion interrogative form is normally polar, expecting the answers 'Yes' or 'No' equally, there can be no exact parallelism between positive and negative inversion questions, the latter in form being directed to eliciting a confirmatory 'No'. Compare the relations between

He knows.	*Does he know?*
He doesn't know.	*Doesn't he know?*

Confronted, therefore, with the instruction to convert *Neither he nor they know the answer* into a question introduced by *do*, some informants chose to construct a question which would in effect be asking for confirmation of the sentence they were converting, while others chose to construct a question to which the sentence as given would correspond as one possible answer. As scrutiny of the results will confirm, twenty-eight chose the former course (basically, *Do neither...?*) and forty-eight the latter and more radical one (basically, *Do either... ?*). Of the twenty-eight who constructed a negative question, twenty-seven retained correlation (twenty-four *neither ... nor*, three *neither ... or*). A little more should be said about the results of the forty-eight informants who constructed a *yes/no* question. *Neither ... nor* is ambiguous as to what is negated, since it may be the negation of the exclusive *either ... or* or of the inclusive *both ... and*. It is rather interesting (though not perhaps surprising, since the *neither ... nor* doubtless gave a bias towards the exclusive interpretation) that only one of the informants formed a *yes/no* question of an inclusive kind: *Do he and they know the answer?*

The selection problem with Test 38 is that of moving in the opposite direction: from the inclusive positive correlation of *Both I and my friend saw the accident*, with the instruction to make the sentence negative. The reaction to the subject-order is dealt with as Operation Test 38 (Ch. 6, p. 78), and we are here concerned only with the ways in which the negation is carried out. It will be seen at once from Table 4 that there is an immediacy in recognising *neither ... nor* as the negative of *both ... and* which is almost completely lacking (as we have seen with Test 47) in recognising *(both) ... and* as one of the possible positive analogues of *neither ... nor*. No less than sixty-two of the informants selected the 'unmarked' negative correlative *neither ... (n)or* in apparent unconcern at its being ambiguous as between exclusive and inclusive. The remaining fourteen informants, however, tried to preserve a markedly inclusive form in the negative too, thirteen by using *both (...) and (...) neg*, the other one by using *(...) and (...) neg + both*. The only other point of interest in the results of Test 38 is the minority correlative form *neither ... or*: four here, as there were three in the Test 47 results. Thus, taking the two tests together, we have: eighty-two *neither ... nor* beside seven *neither ... or*.

The remaining Selection Tests concern three verbs whose negative (and interrogative) forms display divided usage. The first and least complex is Test 35, in which informants were required to supply the negative of *need* corresponding to the positive in *He needs to go at teatime*. Clearly, the preferred form is that of regular open-class verb negation, *do + not + need + to + V* and sixty-one informants supplied this, only one showing signs of hesitation. It was favoured in a ratio of almost 7 : 1 as compared with the only other form which seemed to have any real currency among the informants, nine supplying *need + not + V*, the modal type of negative without the *-s* inflection and without the *to* before the following infinitive; again, one of the informants showed hesitation. Since contracted and uncontracted forms of *not* occurred with both constructions, and since so few selected the modal negative, it was pointless to look for significance as between contraction and non-contraction. Of the remaining informants, four did not perform the negative operation, one selected a blend of the modal and open-class negation (*need + not + to*), and one replaced *need to* by *have to*.

Test 10 concerns the negative of *dare*, and here a preterite form was chosen to test additionally the currency of the uninflected negative form. There are some striking points of similarity with *need*: sixty-one informants used the *do*-auxiliary, eight the modal type of tense-inflected negative, and one a blend without *do* but with *to*. Again, contracted and non-contracted forms of *not* with both the main negation types ruled out any question of significant association. Here the similarity ends, however, and even the degree of similarity mentioned obscures important differences. As Table 4 shows, there is a bigger range of selected forms with *dare* and far more signs of uncertainty (including eight instances of deletion). Two auxiliaries are used (*do* sixty-one times, *would* once), and the auxiliary construction has itself two forms, one with *to* (forty-eight instances), the other without (thirteen instances). The non-auxiliary negative has also two forms, both without a following *to* but differing in tense inflection; while eight informants had the regular tense-inflected *dared*, five used the uninflected variant *dare*.

The negation of *dare* and *need* can now be summed up as follows to bring out the main similarities and differences:

$$
\begin{array}{llll}
aux + neg + dare & \left\langle \begin{array}{l} + \textit{to} \quad 49 \\ + \textit{Ø} \quad 13 \end{array}\right\} & 62 \\[2ex]
aux + neg + need & \left\langle \begin{array}{l} + \textit{to} \quad 61 \\ + \textit{Ø} \quad 0 \end{array}\right\} & 61 \\[2ex]
dare + neg & \left\langle \begin{array}{l} + \textit{to} \quad 1 \\ + \textit{Ø} \quad 13 \end{array}\right\} & \left\{ \begin{array}{l} + \textit{tense} \ 9 \\ - \textit{tense} \ 5 \end{array}\right\} 14 \\[2ex]
need + neg & \left\langle \begin{array}{l} + \textit{to} \quad 1 \\ + \textit{Ø} \quad 9 \end{array}\right\} & 10
\end{array}
$$

In other words, with both verbs there is a roughly 7 : 1 preference for the *do*-negation; with *do*-negation, there is high preference for the *to* construction (absolute with *need*, almost 4 : 1 with *dare*); with modal negation, there is with both verbs an almost absolute preference for the zero construction.

There is one further point of difference that might be mentioned: the shadowy existence of the old preterite *durst* which was used by one informant (though afterwards deleted), as though it had some faint connexion with the negative (since it should be remembered that the given form was already the regular preterite *dared*). In the Quirk and Duckworth experiment (1961), however, the *durst* form was far from shadowy, being used by eight informants a total of fourteen times. This is in fact only one of the notable ways in which the present results contrast with those of the 1961 paper and it is of some importance to compare them. Since the present results relate to seventy-six instances by seventy-six informants and those of 1961 relate to 164 instances by fifty-five informants, the figures are here given in percentages to facilitate comparison:

THE SELECTION TEST

	Present Results		1961 Results	
aux + neg + dare + to	49 (64%)	} 62(82%)	36 (22%)	} 56(34%)
aux + neg + dare + Ø	13 (17%)		20 (12%)	
dared + neg + to	1 (1%)		1 (1%)	
dared + neg + Ø	8 (11%)		59 (36%)	
dare + neg + Ø	5 (7%)	} 13(17%)	34 (21%)	} 107(65%)
durst + neg + Ø	0 (0%)		14 (8%)	

The sharp differences are readily enough attributable to the fact that the informants in the 1961 paper were translating a piece of particularly moving Old English poetry. This not merely confronted them with *dorste* (which helps to explain the 8% use of *durst*, palpably an unfamiliar form since it was three times spelt *darest*, though in colligation with first person), it also motivated an archaic and rhetorical style. The latter is independently attested by inversions like *bend I dared not*. In view of this, it is interesting to find that the modal-type negative (65% as a whole in the 1961 paper) seems more elevated in style than the auxiliary type (34% as a whole in the 1961 paper; 82% in the present experiment). Above all, it is interesting to find such a contrasting distribution of forms available for stylistic purposes, and if the 1961 results are largely skewed by the special circumstances of translating Old English poetry, to what extent are the present results comparably skewed by the special circumstances of impersonal writing (as compared, for example, with personal and familiar speech)?

Finally, there is the selection of forms in the negation of *have*, and here there are two sources of information. Primarily, we have Test 50, which required informants to negate the sentence *I have a black Bentley*. As a secondary source, there is Test 25 in the twenty-three cases where informants converted the negative passive in *A nice little car is had by me* to the negative active. There are four main construction-types:

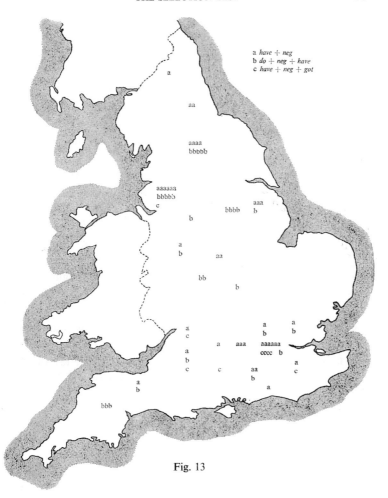

Fig. 13

	Occurrences		
	Test 50	Test 25	Total
(a) *have + neg*	40	8	48
(b) *do + neg + have*	24	12	36
(c) *have + neg + got*	7	3	10
(d) *have + no + N*	4	0	4

With the well-known aspectual exceptions, it is usual to regard (b), the *do*-negation, as a rather rare or non-standard feature in British English. In case any of the tests revealed region-sensitive characteristics, we had – as explained in Chapter 2 – asked informants to state the county in which they had spent all or most of their first fifteen years. Approximately eighty of the main negation types were provided by informants whose early years had been spent in England (in the narrowest regional sense), and the forms were plotted on a map according to the respective counties. As one sees from Fig. 13, there is certainly no obvious regional restriction on the *do*-type of negation; both this form and the modal type of negation are given by informants coming from north, south, east, west, and midland areas. There seems perhaps to be a slightly greater preference for the *do*-type among informants of northerly upbringing. More striking, however, is the distribution of the form *have + neg + got*: of the nine forms recorded by informants from the English counties, eight are by those brought up in the rather narrow area close to a line between the Severn and Thames estuaries.

Unlike the situation with *dare* and *need*, the distribution of contracted and non-contracted forms of *not* in the negation of *have* is by no means random. If we compare first the (a) and (b) negation types for Test 50 in this respect, we have:

		n't	*not*		
(a)	*have + neg*	31	9	40	
(b)	*do + neg + have*	6	18	24	
		37	27	64	$p < .01$

Informants thus showed a clear tendency to use the contracted form with type (a) and the non-contracted form with type (b). As compared with type (c) also, the association of the non-contracted form with type (b) is highly significant:

		n't	*not*		
(b)	*do + neg + have*	6	18	24	
(c)	*have + neg + got*	7	0	7	
		13	18	31	$p = .0007$

The reason for the sharp difference between type (c) and either (a) or (b) in respect of contraction is probably to be found in the stylistic restrictions on (c). This is well-known to be a colloquial form (cf. Gowers, *Fowler's Modern English Usage*, 1965), and it is reasonable that the contraction should persist in its written representation, since a non-contracted *have not got* is little attested in either spoken or written English.

The above tables indicate also a clear difference between type (b) and the other two in respect of contraction, showing a strong association between *do*-negative and non-contraction. The reason in this case may lie in the way informants conceptualised the negative contrast. A sentence and its negative analogue can have identical tonicity:

> *I /saw the wòman#*
> *I /didn't see the wòman#*

But if, on instruction to make a sentence negative, one conceptualises the new form not merely as the negative but as the denial of the original, there is a shift of tonicity. For Test 50, the denial interpretation would give the following forms:

> *I /hàven't a ·black ·Bentley#*
> or   *I do /nòt have a ·black ·Bentley#*

Either of these spoken forms is probably more usual than

> *I have /nòt a ·black ·Bentley#*

Since we have no reason to assume that all informants would adopt the denial possibility, it is likely that many if not most of the other forms elicited in the test represent the simple negative with unshifted tonicity:

> *I have not a /black Bèntley#*
> *I don't have a /black Bèntley#*
> *I haven't got a /black Bèntley#*

Explanation by means of the contrastive denial in this way perhaps accounts for the rather different distribution of negative forms of *have* for Test 25:

	n't	*not*
(a)	3	5
(b)	6	6
(c)	0	3

Although there are considerably fewer instances, and the dangers of inferring too much from them are obvious enough, it is clear that they do not evince the distribution tendencies of the Test 50 results. This could be simply explained by the reduced motivation for denial tonicity-shift since the negative here is doubly removed from the given form, *A nice little car is had by me.*

As we have seen in discussing this last point, the Selection Test in the form developed here has the serious disadvantage of giving only the most indirect indication of the way in which informants would have responded orally; nor can we safely infer their habitual usage in natural speech situations. We have seen earlier, moreover, that it has the defect of eliciting a biased selection by reason of the given form of the sentence, before the operation has been performed, a defect which is of varying gravity with each test and only constant in the insoluble difficulty of assessment that it presents. At the same time, it must also be seen that here is an instrument of great sensitiveness and flexibility for measuring free variation, which achieves a considerable degree of scientific precision and control.

8

CONCLUSION

We have been chiefly concerned in this study with a technique for establishing degrees and kinds of acceptability in English sentences. In view of the defects of the direct-question technique (discussed above in Chapters 1 and 5), we made the basis of our approach an operation technique in which readiness to accept a sentence would be indirectly measured by an informant's ability to replicate its form having duly performed a simple operation on it. One of the grave defects of the direct-question approach – our necessary ignorance of the basis for an informant's judgment – is avoided, and scrutiny of the operation responses can give us very considerable information on the informant's reaction and hence on the types of deviance that sentences manifest. The principle was, therefore, that responses (a) would reveal the specific features, if any, that seemed to give the informant most trouble in the test sentence, and (b) would often indicate positively, by his alteration of the sentence, the usage which the informant preferred. The latter aspect readily lends itself to adaptation for eliciting the range of forms in divided usage or free variation. This is a field in which little work has been done to devise a means of obtaining large amounts of objective, strictly comparable data on features which may be rather rare in occurrence. The Selection Test in our study is an attempt to supply such a means.

With this amount of control over the basis for the informant's reaction, we were then able to use a form of the direct-question approach with its defects removed. As we have seen in Chapter 5, there is some indication of correlation between the Operation and Judgment results as a whole: sentences which had a high Operation success rate tended to be accepted as normal and well-formed in the Judgment Test; those which had a low Operation success rate had likewise a low acceptance rate. But while the judgments of informant groups occur anywhere throughout the entire range between unanimous acceptance and unanimous rejection (the results for the entire population thus giving the interestingly extensive and smooth gradient shown in Fig. 9, p. 52), their ability to perform structural operations has a considerably narrower range of fluctuation; there is seldom a large-scale loss of ability to perceive a linguistic structure, as is shown by the fact that the lowest Operation success score is twenty-three.

In Chapters 4, 6, and 7 we have looked in some detail at the types of result produced by the Operation Test, and these results as a whole would seem to be describable as follows. In the first place, they show the extent to which an informant had trouble performing the operation on a given test sentence. At the 'least trouble' extreme we have complete compliance with the instruction in the Operation Test. Where the results show that an informant had trouble to any extent, small or great, we may next classify them according to whether or not he seemed able to pinpoint a feature that was the source of his unease in the sentence. Where there was evidence of pinpointing, the results could next be classified according to whether or not the informants showed that there was a common or predominant rectification available. Where there was no evidence of pinpointing, the problem was chiefly a lexical one (as in Test 27). Easily rectifiable sentences are classifiable according as the rectifications supplied were grammatical or lexical (an instance of the latter being Test 16). This applies also to the sentences where no common or predominant rectification appeared available, though the distinction is both more difficult to make here and probably less valuable, since in these cases informants tended to treat a given example as either lexical or grammatical. This vacillation itself is a function of the difficulty in rectification; we may compare Tests 15 and 45, discussed in Ch. 4, pp. 44, 46). Easily supplied grammatical rectifications may indicate merest preference (where they are nearest to the 'least trouble' end of the scale, as in Test 36), and from this point they can range downwards to indicate anything from doubtful acceptability (as in Test 14), or unfamiliarity (as in Test 48b), to complete unacceptability (as in Test 26). The rectifications throughout this range can include change of element-order in the test sentence (as in Test 49), replacement of a grammatical item (as in Test 29), addition of a grammatical item (as in Test 39), or change of a grammatical structure (as in Test 25). This classification of the Operation responses can be graphically summarised as in Fig. 14.

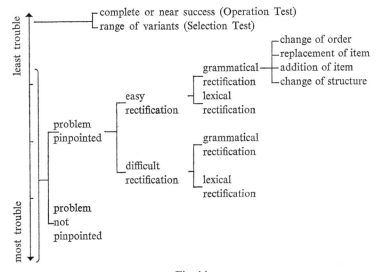

Fig. 14

The Operation and Judgment Tests, then, provide us with two very different but complementary means of estimating relative acceptability, and in the Selection Test we have a means of directly examining preference. The question to be considered now is the bearing that the results of these tests have on the categorial issue raised in Chapter 1. Most obviously and in some ways most importantly, they indicate that clear-cut categorisation is futile and may actually inhibit our understanding of the nature of linguistic acceptability. The absence of a hard and fast line holds even for the distinction between lexical and grammatical acceptability, which as we have seen repeatedly is an inescapable and basic one yet one that is nevertheless liable to be blurred (as in Tests 15 and 45). Moreover, the gradience, readily enough recognised in grammatical usage, persists also within the category of lexical acceptability. From the Operation data alone (Table 2), matrices could be derived demonstrating these characteristics in great detail, and indeed, even in its present form, Table 2 can be regarded as having something of the property of a matrix.

Nevertheless, while we shall bear this gradience in mind in the exposition to follow, we may indicate certain nodes fairly confidently in a general framework:

I: LEXICAL	II: GRAMMATICAL
(a) congruous	(a) established
(b) obscure	(b) divided
(c) incoherent	(c) ill-established
	(d) dubious
	(e) unacceptable

I(a): This category accommodates most of the sentences in the test battery, irrespective of the gross success or acceptance scores in the Operation and Judgment Tests. What is crucial is that there should be no F- or H-type failures in the Operation Test; this is equally true for Tests 2, 35, 38, 29, 24, to quote only a few examples with sharp differences in other respects. The classification of the Operation Test results thus interestingly provides for the independence of lexis from grammar, inasmuch as a sentence can be grammatically highly deviant without being regarded as lexically deviant.

I(b): In this category, the lexical relations cause sufficient resistance for the sentences to score low acceptability results in the Judgment Test but not sufficient to prevent a reasonably high success score in the Operation Test; for example, Tests 16 and 41. The category includes sentences whose problem some informants feel to be lexical and others grammatical (as in Tests 15 and 45), and thus contrasts with category I(a) in showing the interdependence of lexical deviance and grammatical deviance. It would seem that it is to this category that lexical deviance of a metaphorical

or figurative kind is to be referred, and the viability of a figurative
lexical relation perhaps accounts for the degree of Operation success achieved with Test 41. Such an area of deviance is least susceptible to satisfactory study by means of isolated sentences. Even
in relation to grammar itself, 'stripping a sentence to its minimum ... is a risky test of grammaticality: it often falsifies the
potentialities of the construction' (Bolinger, 1961, 377); with
lexical relations, the potentialities are obviously still more sharply
and easily falsified. If it were textually embedded in such a sequence as

> *Day was over and the shadows were lengthening as I*
> *approached the forest; dusk was creeping up between*
> *the trees.*

there can be little doubt that Test 16 would have both a high success and a high acceptance score. While this shows that other
tests must be developed for a fuller exploration of the 'obscure'
category, the validity of the present categorisation and the type
of test on which it is based are alike confirmed by the fact that
on this basis an important collocational difference can be demonstrated between *dusk* + *creep* and (say) *child* + *creep*.

I(c): In this category, we have not only low acceptance scores
in the Judgment Test but a scatter of failure types in the Operation
Test suggesting a deviance so great that many informants could
not perceive any structure, lexical or grammatical. The results
of Test 27 (discussed in Ch. 4, p. 44) amply illustrate the fact that
a lexically deviant sentence cannot be perceived as grammatically
non-deviant and may be perceived as entirely incoherent. As
with the 'obscurity' of I(b), so with the 'incoherence' of the present
category, the classification is relative to a degree of textual isolation
that allows the category I(a) to emerge. Even *Friendship dislikes
John* could doubtless be contextualised so as to be perceived as
coherent, but that does not make it lexically congruous (compare
the discussion of *Golf plays John* in Chomsky, 1961, 234f.).

II(a): In this category we place sentences given a high success and a high acceptance score: for example, Test 1 and the other 'control' sentences discussed at the beginning of Chapter 4. On this basis, all sentences classed as II(a) must also be classed as I(a), emphasising the primacy of lexical congruence, since, as we have seen, a sentence is not perceived as grammatically non-deviant (that is, there will be G- or I-type failures) if it is lexically deviant.

II(b): By 'divided usage' we understand competing forms which are acceptable and, broadly speaking, equally so. Sentences are therefore assigned to this category partly on the basis of approximate parity in the Operation and Judgment scoring, with fairly high success and acceptance results, and partly on the evidence that informants make changes to introduce both the competing forms. The most direct evidence comes of course in the results of the Selection Test. Examples are Tests 11 and 36 (see above, Ch. 6, pp. 76f.), where there is switching from *whom* to *who* and from *who* to *whom* in identical grammatical environments. The effect of many generations of prescriptive tradition in grammar teaching is to some extent felt in this category (in preventing, for example, either of the competing forms from winning unanimous acceptance), as also in the next.

II(c): This category embraces structures of various types brought together only by the fact that rules governing their form and use appear not to be well established among users of the language. Examples may include minority competitive forms that might otherwise seem indistinguishable from those in divided usage (for example, Tests 7 and 17); structures of the kind mentioned on p. 11, for which through unfamiliarity, rarity, or complexity, or a combination of these, native speakers seem to lack a clear *Sprachgefühl* (for example, Test 34 and the correlative construction in Test 47); structures in which there happens to be no 'right' usage – the situation that we obviously have in the variants given in Table 4 for Test 22. The score characteristics for this category are a fairly high acceptance level in the Judgment Test and a scatter of results in the Operation or Selection Tests.

II(d): Tests 6 and 39 would seem to be good examples of a

category labelled 'dubious'. The Operation success rate is only fair and few informants are prepared to make acceptance responses in the Judgment Test. On the other hand, there is not a majority for rejecting the sentences, and a fairly large number of informants register 'query' responses. A rather wide range of sentence acceptability should probably be recognised here, from the mild discomfort evidenced in the results for Test 6 to the acute dislike of Test 44 (thirty-nine Operation successes, four Judgment acceptances), which closely approaches complete rejection as ungrammatical.

II(e): In this category we place sentences which (as the results suggest) could scarcely be uttered naturally by a native speaker except as a *lapsus linguae* or a joke: Tests 5 and 25, for example, with their extremely low success and acceptance rates. It would of course also include the sentences like *Little a boy the ran street up* which, though never perhaps 'mouthed by poet or peasant', have tended to be taken in recent years as the type of the ungrammatical sentence.

The test techniques which have been described in this study and which have resulted in the foregoing typology of acceptability are inadequate in many ways. It was a mistaken economy to combine two test problems in a single test sentence (as in 23a and 23b, 48a and 48b), thereby losing the check provided by the Judgment Test (see Ch. 6, pp. 73f.). Even in conjunction with the Operation Test, the basis for the informants' responses in the Judgment Test can remain doubtful (as we saw, for example, in the discussion of Test 12, Ch. 5, pp. 63f.). A test technique which yielded oral instead of written results would remove other undesirable ambiguities (as we saw in relation to the selected forms for Test 50 on pp. 94 ff.), and would in any case have obvious independent advantages; we have noted from time to time points at which preferences no doubt vary between speech and writing (for example, Ch. 6, p. 77). A means must be found of evaluating Operation results in respect of sentences differing sharply in rectifiability but not necessarily in acceptability. For example, the success score of fifty-five for Test 3 is obviously not directly comparable

with that of thirty-nine for Test 44, though the technique of analysing non-successes already in part offsets the falsifying tendencies of the success figures in isolation.

Further work is clearly necessary not merely to eliminate the
present defects but also to explore the many promising possibilities
that we have scarcely been able to touch upon. Plans are already in
hand to experiment with oral responses to such a test battery
through the use of a language laboratory. Thereby (it is hoped),
we should retain the advantages of the present technique in so far as
they concern simultaneous application of the tests to numbers of
informants, while obviating the defects noted in written responses;
we should also procure additional enlightening data which could
sharpen the scoring and classification procedure. We would claim,
however, that the method of investigation has already justified
itself even in the few test results presented in this study, and that
it has a contribution to make in the scientific control that it offers
for inquiry into an area of linguistics as important as it is complex.

TABLES

TAB

		Test Details			Group I Results	
No.	Operation	Instr. Order[a]	Test sentence	Op. Success[b]	Judgment +	?
1	inversion question	os	They/always còme here #	28	28	0
2	present	os	/Jack admired sincèrity #	27	26	2
3	inv. qu. I neg. II	so	I was/sat opposite by a strànger #	18	0	10
4	past	so	He/wants some càke #	27	28	0
5	inv. qu.	so	/John works there èither #	18	0	0
6	positive	so	He/isn't much lòved #	22	15	10
7	plural	so	It's in the/front of the stàtion #	20	23	3
8	inv. qu.	so	You/painted your fence blùe #	28	27	0
9	singular	so	They/ăren't # but they pre/tènd to be #	24	26	2
10	negative	so	He/dared to answer me bàck #	S	26	2
−11	present	os	/Whom did you sèe #	26	16	9
12	inv. qu.	os	He is/silly and crỳing #	8	9	16
13[c]	present	os	Neither/he nor I knew the ànswer #	26 S	26	1
14	plural	os	He is re/garded insàne #	23	9	10
15	inv. qu.	os	/Food was lacked by the children #	20	6	9
16	present	os	/Dusk was creeping up between the trèes #	23	21	4
17	negative	os	The/old man chose his son a wife #	25	15	8
−18	inv. qu.	os	It's the/man to whom I spòke #	22	21	4
19	present	os	We pro/vided the man a drìnk #	23	7	9
20	singular	os	They/own a large fàctory #	28	27	1
21	past	so	I/turn on the light for the room to look brìghter #	19	16	11
22[c]	present	so	Neither/I nor he felt a thing #	20 S	20	4
23[c]	past	so	He/turns to the [misiz] Smìth #	a26 b17	15	6
24	inv. qu.	so	They/painted blue their dòor #	12	4	4
25[c]	negative	so	A/nice little car is had by mè #	15 (S)	1	1
26	inv. qu.	so	/He sits àlways there #	12	2	6
27	past	so	/Friendship dislikes Jòhn #	22	2	3
28	posit. I negat. II	so	The/woman sat òpposite me #	28	26	1
29	past	so	They/don't want some càke #	24	6	6
30	inv. qu.	so	/Bill comes here tòo #	28	28	0

ss^b	roup II Results — Judgment +	?	−	Op. Success^b		Conflation — Judgment +	?	−	Percentage — Operation Success^b I	II	I&II	Judgment (+ only) I	II	I&II
	47	1	0	75		75	1	0	100	98	99	100	98	99
	42	5	1	75		68	7	1	96	100	99	93	88	89
	0	5	43	55		0	15	61	64	77	72	0	0	0
	48	0	0	74		76	0	0	96	98	97	100	100	100
	0	1	47	40		0	1	75	64	46	53	0	0	0
	7	31	10	63		22	41	13	79	85	83	54	15	29
	30	16	2	49		53	19	4	71	60	65	82	63	70
	45	3	0	74		72	3	1	100	96	97	96	94	95
	41	7	0	68		67	9	0	86	92	89	93	85	88
S	44	3	1		S	70	5	1				93	92	92
	39	5	4	60		55	14	7	93	71	79	57	81	72
	15	23	10	34		24	39	13	29	52	45	32	31	32
S	42	4	2	74	S	68	5	3	93	100	97	93	88	89
	11	22	15	60		20	32	24	82	77	79	32	23	26
	9	20	19	57		15	29	32	71	77	75	21	19	20
	20	14	14	57		41	18	17	82	71	75	75	42	54
	16	16	16	69		31	24	21	89	92	91	54	33	41
	35	10	3	58		56	14	6	79	75	76	75	73	74
	8	19	21	45		15	28	33	82	46	59	25	17	20
	46	2	0	75		73	3	0	100	98	99	96	96	96
	20	12	16	42		36	23	17	68	48	55	57	42	47
S	36	8	4	56	S	56	12	8	71	75	74	71	75	74
	16	16	16	a74		31	22	23	a93	100	97	54	33	41
				b34					b61	35	45			
	0	10	38	26		4	14	58	43	29	34	14	0	5
(S)	0	1	47	36	(S)	1	2	73	53	44	47	4	0	1
	0	1	47	23		2	7	67	43	23	30	7	0	3
	3	4	41	60		5	7	64	79	79	79	7	6	7
	47	0	1	74		73	1	2	100	96	97	93	98	96
	10	19	19	49		16	25	35	86	52	65	21	21	21
	46	2	0	73		74	2	0	100	94	96	100	96	97

(continued)

	Test Details			Group I Results	
No.	Operation	Instr. Order[a]	Test sentence	Op. Success[b]	Judgmen + ?
31	plural	so	It's in/front of the còllege #	28	28 0
32	positive	os	They/aren't very lòved #	18	2 7
33	inv. qu.	os	They/pushed the gate òpen #	28	27 1
34	singular	os	They/ăren't # but they/clàim so #	26	12 8
35	negative	os	He/needs to go at tèatime #	S	22 5
36	present	os	/Who did you wànt #	26	21 4
37	inv. qu.	os	She is/clever and prètty #	27	27 0
38[c]	negative	os	Both/I and my friend saw the àccident #	27 S	22 4
39	plural	os	I re/gard him fòolish #	23	4 11
40	inv. qu.	os	/Clothing was needed by the pòor #	28	21 6
41	present	os	I /Wood ⎫ was creeping II/Timber ⎭ up the hìll #	26	6 5
42	negative	os	A/wife was chosen his sòn #	13	3 1
43	inv. qu.	os	It's the/girl I spòke to #	26	28 0
44	present	os	Some/food was provided the màn #	19	4 3
45	singular	so	They are/owning hundreds of àcres #	16	4 8
46	past	so	I/stop the car for the children to get òut #	27	25 2
47	inv. qu.	so	Neither/he nor they know the ànswer #	S	23 5
48[c]	past	so	The/Miss Browns are tùrned to #	b25 a24	7 3
49	inv. qu.	so	He/pushed open the dòor #	24	26 2
50	negative	so	I have a/black Bèntley #	S	27 1

	Group II Results			Conflation				Percentage					
	Judgment			Op. Success[b]	Judgment			Operation Success[b]			Judgment (+ only)		
ss[b]	+	?	−		+	?	−	I	II	I&II	I	II	I&II
	48	0	0	74	76	0	0	100	96	97	100	100	100
	2	13	33	49	4	20	52	64	65	65	7	4	5
	46	2	0	73	73	3	0	100	94	96	96	96	96
	21	21	6	71	33	29	14	93	94	93	43	44	43
S	37	8	3	S	59	13	4				79	77	78
	42	2	4	67	63	6	7	93	85	88	75	88	83
	42	6	0	72	69	6	1	96	94	95	96	88	91
S	35	10	3	70 S	57	14	5	96	90	92	79	73	75
	8	20	20	56	12	31	33	82	69	74	14	17	16
	41	6	1	76	62	12	2	100	100	100	75	85	82
	11	5	32	72	17	10	49	93	96	95	21	23	22
	0	4	44	48	3	5	68	46	73	63	11	0	4
	40	5	3	60	68	5	3	93	71	79	100	83	89
	0	8	40	39	4	11	61	68	42	51	14	0	5
	16	17	15	35	20	25	31	57	40	46	14	33	26
	42	5	1	71	67	7	2	96	92	94	89	88	88
S	30	11	7	S	53	16	7				82	63	70
	3	16	29	b61 a57	10	19	47	b89 a86	75 69	80 75	25	6	13
	34	11	3	57	60	13	3	86	69	75	93	71	82
S	47	0	1	S	74	1	1				96	98	97

os = announcement of required operation followed by announcement of sentence; so = converse.

Operation Success = 'A' set scores: see Tables 2 and 3.

13, 22, and 38 are scored as Operation tests in respect of the order of the elements operating as subject; 25 is scored as a Selection test where the passive is replaced by active; 23 and 48 are scored as two Operation tests, (b) relating to 'the Misses Smith' and 'the Miss Browns' respectively.

Selection tests; see Selection Test Table (Table 4).

110

TABLE 2 *Operation Test Table: De...*

Pattern set	Pattern number	A	B	C	D	E	F	G	H	I	J	K	41	9	17	46	34	38	36	6	48b
A	1	×											67	67	51	68	63	65	66	55	48
	2	×	+										1					6	2		
	3	×		+									2	1	10		5		1	3	5
	4	×	+	+																	
	5	×			+								2	2			4				1
	6	×				+												1	1	4	5
	7	×	+			+															
	8	×		+		+															
	9	×			+	+															2
	10	×		+	+		+														
	11	×						+							3					1	
	12	×								+											
	13	×				+				+											
	14	×		+		+				+											
F (in GHIK)	15						×						1	1	1						
	16		+				×							(1)							
G (in HI)	17							×					3	6	1	1	1				
	18		+					×													
	19			+				×													
	20				+			×													
	21					+		×													
	22		+			+		×													
	23						+	×													
	24		+				+	×					1	(1)						(3)	
H (in IJK)	25								×												
	26		+						×												
	27			+					×												
	28				+				×												
	29					+			×												
	30						+		×												
	31						+	+	×					(1)							(1)

)ective Scores

6	15	11	27	48a	39	49	22	3	32	42	29	7	19	44	21	5	25	45	12	23b	24	26	Totals
8	52	52	44	46	49	54	46	42	44	36	39	45	39	30	41	32	31	26	28	24	26	21	1603
3								2		1	2	2		3			3	2	2	1	1		35
4	3	7	1		2	3	3	2	3	9	4	1	4	1	1	1	1	2				1	85
							1			2			1	1									5
2	1		11	3						1	2				1			3					36
1	1	3	11	1			5	3		1	4				1		3	1	3	3	9	1	66
										1													1
			1												1								3
																							3
																		1					1
							5																9
								1						2	1								5
										1													1
											1												1
		3														3		1				1	15
		1																					1
	(2)	(2)					(1)	(2)								(1)		(1)	(4)				
2	3	3	1	4	5	2	1			6	1				1		8	2	5				72
								1							1								3
									1		1												5
		1																					1
								1															1
																		1					1
								1			1												2
																							1
(2)		(3)			(1)			(2)	(2)	(1)	(4)		(2)	(3)	(2)	(5)	(1)	(2)	(2)	(2)		(1)	
3	6	1					1	3							1			1	8				34
	1	1																					2
2								1															3
																		1					1
								1															1
1								1		1			1							1			4
																			1				1
	(1)	(1)						(3)		(1)			(1)					(2)	(1)				

(continued)

Pattern set	Pattern number	A	B	C	D	E	F	G	H	I	J	K	41	9	17	46	34	38	36	6	48b1
I	32									×			2	2	4	6	9	6	8	1	
	33		+							×											1
	34			+						×			1	1							1
	35		+	+						×											
	36				+					×											
	37					+				×										4	1
	38		+			+				×											
	39			+		+				×											
	40				+	+				×											
	41						+			×											
	42			+			+			×											
	43							+		×										3	
	44		+					+		×											
	45					+		+		×			1								
	46		+			+		+		×											
	47						+	+		×											
	48								+	×			1								1
(in JK)														(1)							
J	49								×												
(in K)	50						+		×												
	51							+	×												
K	52										×										3
	53								+		×				1						
	54	+							+		×										
	55				+				+		×										
	56				+	+			+		×										
	57							+	+		×										
	58									+	×										

ctive Scores

	15	11	27	48a	39	49	22	3	32	42	29	7	19	44	21	5	25	45	12	23b	24	26	Totals
	6	6		8	11	12	15	10	16	11	21	20	21	23	22	18	19	18	25	40	43	52	473
					1					1	1					2			1				8
	1					2		1		1	1		5	4		1	1		2		3		27
													1	2									3
		1		1																			3
	2	1				2	1	2	2	1	1	3		4		1	1	6	3	2	3		41
																1		1					2
								1															1
										1													1
		1														1		3					5
		1																					1
		3		1				2	4	1	2	1	4	1	3	1	1		1				30
													1	1									2
		1				1				1			1										5
									1														1
						1																	1
				1	1				1				1		1	1							8
					(4)	(1)		(1)		(3)					(1)	(6)	(2)		(1)				
								1							1								2
									3														3
																	1						1
								(1)		(1)						(2)	(2)						
				6	4										1	2	1						17
					1					2					1	5							11
										1													1
																1							1
					1			1											1				2
																	1						1
								1		1						2	2						7
																							2660

TABLE 3

Operation Test Results grouped by Pattern-Set Totals

Pattern sets	Grouped Test Numbers and Respective Scores							Totals
	1 41 9 17 46 34 38 36	**2** 6 48b 14 43	**3** 18 16 15 11 27	**4** 48a 39 49 22 3 32 42 29	**5** 7 19 44 21	**6** 5 25 45 12	**7** 23b 24 26	
A	72 68 69 71 71 70 67	63 61 59 60	58 57 57 60 57	56 57 56 55 49 49 49 49	45 39 42 40	36 35 34 34	26 23	1854
F	1 1 1 (1)		4 (2) (2)	(1) (2)	3 (1)	1 (1) (4)	1	16
G	3 7 1 1 1 (1)	(3)	9 11 2 3 3 (1) (2) (4)	3 5 6 2 2 1 6 7 1 (1) (2) (2) (1) (4) (1) (2) (3) (2) (5) (1) (4) (2) (2)	1 1 (1)	1 8 3 5 (2) (2) (1)		92
H	(1)		16 7 2 (1) (1) (1)	1 1 1 (3) (1)		1 10 1 (1) (2) (1)		40
I	5 3 4 6 9 13 12 16 6 3 (1)	3 1 (1)	9 13 1 9 14 17 18 16 18 17 25 27 30 35 (1) (3)	28 25 26 27 35 42 50 52 (1) (6) (2) (1)				612
J		(1)		1 3 (1)	1 (1)	1 1 (2) (2)		6
K	1	3 1 1	6 5	2	3 1	2 10 4	1	40
								2660

TABLE 4

Test number	Range of variants	Group I				Group II				Conflation			
		Total selected	simply selected	selected hesitantly[a]	selected then deleted	Total selected	simply selected	selected hesitantly[a]	selected then deleted	Total selected	simply selected	selected hesitantly[a]	selected then deleted
13	know	20	19	1	1	33	31	2	1	53	50	3	2
	knows	8	7	1	1	14	13	1	1	22	20	2	2
	knows & know					1	1			1	1		
22	he feel	12	10	2	1	24	19	5	1	36	29	7	2
	he feels	9	8	1	2	11	10	1	4	20	18	2	6
	I feel	6	6			7	6	1		13	12	1	
	I feels					3	3			3	3		
	I do not feel nor does he					1	1			1	1		
	I, nor he, feel					1	1			1	1		
	he are feeling	1	1							1	1		
	(wrong operation)					1				1			
47	do neither he nor they	11	7	4		12	8	4		23	15	8	
	do either he or they	9	6	3		17	15	2	4	26	21	5	2
	do neither he or they	2	1	1						2	1	1	
	do either him or they					1		1		1		1	
	do either him or them					1		1		1		1	
	do he and they					1	1			1	1		
	do either they or he					1		1		1		1	
	do they or he	1	1			2	1	1		3	2	1	
	do they are he					1	1			1	1		
	do they or him								1				1
	do either of them					3	2	1	1	3	2	1	1
	do any of them					1		1		1		1	
	do neither of you					1	1			1	1		
	does neither he nor they	1	1		3				1	1	1		4
	does neither he or they					1	1			1	1		
	does either he or they	2	2			2	2		1	4	4		1
	does he or they	1	1		1	3	2	1		4	3	1	1
	does either him or they								1				1
	does either they or he								1				1
	do they know or does he know					1		1		1		1	
	does either he or do they	1	1							1	1		
	do(es) ... knows								2				2

[a] This refers to evidence of hesitation over the problem centre only.

Test number	Range of variants	Group I				Group II				Conflation			
		Total selected	simply selected	selected hesitantly[a]	selected then deleted	Total selected	simply selected	selected hesitantly[a]	selected then deleted	Total selected	simply selected	selected hesitantly[a]	selected then deleted
38	neither x nor y	21	19	2		37	34	3		58	53	5	
	both x and y + negative	6	6		2	7	7		2	13	13		4
	neither x or y					4	4			4	4		
	x and y didn't both	1	1							1	1		
10	didn(o)t dare to	18	14	4	1	30	30			48	44	4	1
	didn(o)t dare Ø	6	5	1		7	6	1		13	11	2	
	dared not Ø	4	4		3b	4	4		1	8			4
	dare not Ø					5	5		1	5	5		1
	durstn't Ø				1								1
	wouldn(o)t dare to					1	1			1	1		
	dared not to				1	1	1	1		1		1	1
35	doesn(o)t need to	23	23		1	38	37	1		61	60	1	1
	needn(o)t Ø	3	2	1		6	6			9	8	1	
	doesn(o)t have to					1	1			1	1		
	needn(o)t to					1	1			1	1		
	(wrong operation)	2				2				4			
50	have not	3	2	1	1	6	6		2	9	8	1	3
	haven't	11	10	1		20	17	3		31	27	4	
	do not have	5	4	1		13	12	1		18	16	2	
	don't have	2	2			4	4		1	6	6		1
	have not got				1								1
	haven't got	4	4			3	3			7	7		
	have no	3	3			1	1			4	4		
	(wrong operation)					1				1			
25	have not	1	1			3	3			4	4		
	haven't	1	1			2	2			3	3		
	do not have	1	1			3	2	1		4	3	1	
	don't have	1	1			2	2			3	3		
	have not got					3	3			3	3		
	had not	1	1							1	1		
	did not have					2	2			2	2		
	didn't have					3	3			3	3		

b A single instance of "dar" is arbitrarily included here.

REFERENCES

Bach, E., *An Introduction to Transformational Grammars* (New York, 1964).
Bolinger, D. L., "Linguistic Science and Linguistic Engineering", *Word*, 16 (1960), 374-91.
——, "Syntactic Blends and Other Matters", *Lg.*, 37 (1961), 366-81.
Chomsky, N., *Syntactic Structures* (The Hague, 1957).
——, "Some Methodological Remarks on Generative Grammar", *Word*, 17 (1961), 219-39.
——, *Aspects of the Theory of Syntax* (Cambridge, Mass., 1965).
Crystal, D. & Quirk, R., *Systems of Prosodic and Paralinguistic Features in English* (The Hague, 1964).
Finney, D. J., Latscha, R., Bennett, B. M., & Hsu, P., *Tables for Testing Significance in a 2 x 2 Contingency Table* (Cambridge, 1963).
Hays, D. G., "Dependency Theory: A Formalism and Some Observations", *Lg.*, 40 (1964), 511-25.
Hill, A. A., "Grammaticallity", *Word*, 17 (1961), 1-10.
Katz, J. J., "Semi-sentences", in *The Structure of Language*, ed. by J. A. Fodor and J. J. Katz (Englewood Cliffs, N. J., 1964), pp. 400-16.
Lambek, J., "On the Calculus of Syntactic Types", *Proceedings of Symposia in Applied Mathematics* (Providence), 12 (1961), 166-78.
Maclay, H. & Sleator, M. D., "Responses to Language: Judgments of Grammaticalness", *IJAL*, 26 (1960), 275-82.
Miller, G. A. & Isard, S., "Some Perceptual Consequences of Linguistic Rules", *Journal of Verbal Learning and Verbal Behavior*, 2 (1963), 217-28.
Putnam, H., "Some Issues in the Theory of Grammar", *Proceedings of Symposia in Applied Mathematics* (Providence), 12 (1961), 25-42.
Quirk, R., "Descriptive Statement and Serial Relationship", *Lg.*, 41 (1965), 205-17.
Quirk, R. & Duckworth, A. P., "Co-existing Negative Preterite Forms of *dare*", *Language and Society: A. M. Jensen Festschrift* (Copenhagen, 1961), pp. 135-40.
Quirk, R. & Mulholland, J., "Complex Prepositions and Related Sequences", Supplement to *English Studies*, 45 (1964), 64-73.
Svartvik, J., "A Note on *for* plus Infinitive", *English Language Teaching*, 19 (1965), 134-6.
——, *On Voice in the English Verb* (The Hague, 1966).
Twaddell, W. F., *The English Verb Auxiliaries*, 2nd ed. (Providence, 1963).
Ziff, P., "About Ungrammaticalness", *Mind*, 73 (1964), 204-14.
Zimmer, K. E., *Affixal Negation in English and Other Languages*, Supplement to *Word*, 20 (1964).

JANUA LINGUARUM

STUDIA MEMORIAE NICOLAI VAN WIJK DEDICATA

Edited by Cornelis H. van Schooneveld

SERIES MINOR

MOUTON & CO · PUBLISHERS · THE HAGUE

2-102